D1413737

30 WAYS
TO NURTURE YOUR CHILD'S SPIRIT AND ENRICH YOUR FAMILY'S LIFE

PARENTING
with Spirit

by JANE BARTLETT

MJF BOOKS
NEW YORK

Published by MJF Books
Fine Communications
322 Eighth Avenue
New York, NY 10001

Parenting with Spirit
LC Control Number 2006938834
ISBN-13: 978-1-56731-867-8
ISBN-10: 1-56731-867-3

Copyright © 2004 by Jane Bartlett
Foreword Copyright © 2004 by Steve Biddulph

This edition is published by MJF Books in arrangement with Marlowe &
Company, a Division of Avalon Publishing Group, Inc.

All rights reserved. No part of this publication may be reproduced or transmit-
ted in any form or by any means, electronic or mechanical, including photo-
copy, recording, or any information storage and retrieval system, without the
prior written permission of the publisher.

Printed in the United States of America.

MJF Books and the MJF colophon are trademarks of Fine Creative Media, Inc.

QM   10 9   8   7   6   5   4   3   2   1

To my husband John, and my children Benedict, Dominic, and Iona, without whom this spiritual journey would not have been possible. With my gratitude and love.

Contents

CONTENTS

Foreword

STEVE BIDDULPH

WE WANT OUR children to grow up happy, healthy, strong, and kind. But that isn't what the world wants. The world wants them greedy, insecure, selfish, shallow, and vain—to eat this junk food, buy those clothes, watch this TV show, crave that magazine. Never knowing peace or feeling satisfaction. So, almost from the minute you first cradle your baby in your arms, you are at war.

But rather than a war of aggression, you have better tools at your disposal. You have love and patience, and a sense of right and wrong; you have laughter and the strength that comes from having good friends to encourage you. You have the peace that comes from appreciating nature and from knowing that joy comes from the inside, not from what you own—not from insurance policies or double glazing or holiday resorts where they mind the kids.

So what is Spirit? When a small child draws a tree, the drawing will probably look like a lollipop plonked on the ground. We adults know otherwise—that there are deep and enormous root systems under that tree, and within the tree there are complex and beautiful processes that drink sunshine, draw up water, and purify air. We know that life has an inside story, a richer reality than whatever shows on the surface. We know that old and wrinkled are beautiful, that slow and careful are valuable, that time to smile and talk is wealth. That nothing lives or breathes or moves on the earth without being united in the deep spirit and energy of being that most of the world calls God.

But there—I've used it—the "G" word! And closely related, the "R" word: religion. Religion may not be for everyone but it can provide a context and a community of people that our children can draw on, perhaps imperfect but rich and challenging. When we have just a few brief years in this life, it so much helps to tap into the millions of people who have lived their lives before us, built those traditions and made those pathways on which we can seek our liberation. Since our kids learn not from our words but from our deeds, we need all the help we can get. So whether you have a tradition, or can find one, or would rather just make your own, this book can help.

Because this is the big one. Spirit isn't something you can add to your life like exercise or cooking classes. It's the inside of everything you do—your love for your child and how you show it; the things you take a stand on; the big choices you make about time, money, and faithfulness in your marriage; about going out in the cold to check on your elderly neighbor, opposing war, or refusing to let fear be the driving force in our national life.

Jane Bartlett makes no pretense of being an expert. She is like all of us—muddling along, but determined to get better. So she has gathered a wide and eclectic range of everyday tools that are far from everyday in their effect: they are doorways for our children and for us to pass through into the timeless and potent world of the sacred, where life comes from and goes to, and where we can be whole and healed in a broken world.

STEVE BIDDULPH,
author of *The Secret of Happy Children*

Introduction

IS THERE SOMETHING missing from your family life?

It may seem on the surface that there is nothing missing at all. How could there be? The modern lifestyle we create with our children is busy and full, and it's hard to imagine a day when we might squeeze anything else in. There's the school run, the swimming lessons, the ballet classes, homework, Saturday morning soccer games, violin practice, the birthday parties, the medical appointments, the camping trips, the latest children's book or film to read or see. We parents, when not navigating our children's schedule, may be holding down a demanding job, running a home, and trying to have a social and leisure life of our own. We might struggle to get the right balance between work, rest, and play, but surely there can be nothing missing? Yet despite this apparent richness of activity, I believe many of us feel that something has been forgotten.

We catch sight of it sometimes, in those small, quiet moments when we transcend our daily whirl, as if we have entered the eye of the storm. It comes to us when, as we close the nursery curtains, we glimpse the celestial night sky. It comes to us when we see our children asleep in bed, their angelic faces frozen in the darkness. It comes to us when we weep while watching the school nativity play. It often takes us by surprise, suddenly knocking at our hearts, when we feel a small hand slip itself into our solid grip; or when chopping vegetables we hear the froth of children's laughter floating in from the yard.

And we feel its absence too. Something is missing when all the Christmas presents have been unwrapped, the food devoured, and one too many videos watched. Something is missing when our child is feverish in bed and all we find ourselves able to do is watch and administer cold washcloths. Something is missing when our child asks us "Where do I come from?" and we only talk factually about eggs, sperm, and babies in tummies.

What is it that we catch sight of? What is it that we sometimes miss? It is the sacred, that deeper draft of life that belongs to us all, children and adults, whether we are religious or not. It has been known around the world throughout the ages by a hundred different names: Brahman, Tao, Yahweh, Spirit, the Divine, Nirvana, the Goddess, the Source, Universal Energy, the ground of being, Lord, Allah, Higher Self, God. In the midst of all the doing of parenting, we are unexpectedly shot through with a moment of being, a delivery of divine grace, a deep knowing about what is splendid and enduring. Daily our children seem to dance and sing out to us of its very existence, yet often we do very little about it within our family life. It's rarely acknowledged, encouraged, or celebrated, but remains an ember that fails to burn brightly because it is never fanned. That is how it is for many of us today.

A NEW SPIRITUALITY

In the past we would have taken our children to church, synagogue, mosque, or temple, and relied upon the worship found there to anchor a spiritual awareness in our family lives. However, we all know that organized religion is currently in decline. Surveys consistently show that at least two-thirds of us profess to some sort of belief in a supreme being, but only around 8 percent go to church. A report by Anglican researchers published in 2002 called "Hope for the Church" predicted that by 2030 there will be practically no children in church if the current trend continues. Census figures in Australia show that many Christian congregations are in decline, some by as much as 22 percent. In Canada, census figures also show a continued drift away from organized religion, with the number of people who say they have no religion up by nearly 44 percent between 1991 and 2001. The picture is different in the United States., where statistics suggest that 43 percent of adults (mainly in the South and Midwest) attend church, but even here there has been a small decline since 1991.

The discontent with institutionalized religion is widely held: many view it as dogmatic, misogynistic, homophobic, not credible to twenty-first-century thinkers, boring. Nevertheless there is still a spiritual hunger, and we are engaged in an effort to find new ways in which it can be satisfied. Into the vacuum being created by the demise of organized religion comes a growing New Age movement, neopaganism, an interest in the spiritual practices of indigenous peoples, personal development, and an enthusiasm for holistic living. The West is embracing Eastern spirituality in the belief that it is more rational and less rule-bound than Christianity. Christianity too now has its movements that are committed to a progressive interpretation of the faith and a rediscovery of its spiritual core, letting go of traditional dogmas that, to twenty-first-century eyes, now look more like expressions of culture than eternal truths.

We live in changing times, but so far this spiritual renaissance has largely failed to nurture families. It concerns itself only with the needs of grown-ups; it's individualistic and self-orientated. You will find a wealth of personal development opportunities for adults to discover their "inner child," but few where they can be with their outer child too! I can remember, after many years' involvement with many of the previously mentioned spiritual movements, I suddenly found myself set apart and stranded as soon as I had a baby in my arms. All those interesting lectures, courses, workshops, acts of worship, meditation, and prayer groups that I used to attend were now barred to the "me" that had become an "us." Life got even more difficult when I had a baby and a toddler, and impossible when it was a baby, a toddler, and a preschooler. Finding a like-minded spiritual community where we could all be together as a family has been a momentous challenge, and this book is largely born out of that frustration.

SPIRITUALITY FOR FAMILIES

How can we as parents cultivate our own spirituality amid the frenzy of our lives? And, just as importantly, how do we nurture our children's spiritual development too? If we don't feel we can go to church or belong to another organized religion, and we can't take the kids along to the local meditation group or New Age workshop, what do we do? I believe the answer for many is, nothing. We do nothing. The sacred moments in our life are rare, and our children, who in many ways are far more tuned into the awe and miraculous aspects of life than adults, are little souls left to wander.

We are anxious about how dispersed and fragile families have become in recent years, about how the lives of parents and children have become faster and overscheduled. We mourn the loss of the family meal, a potent symbol of family connection. We worry about all the negative influences that may come into our children's lives and our ability as parents to prepare them for what is harsh. Developing a family spirituality does not mean that siblings will no longer squabble, that the toddler will no longer have a tantrum, or that your eight-year-old will suddenly become fantastically compliant—these are the normal problems of family life—but it will help you deal with these difficulties as they arise, and give you a powerful means of restoring harmony.

Families need to find their spiritual heart if they are to flourish in the new millennium. For this to happen, religious communities must become much more welcoming and appealing. That is not the subject of this book, but it is important work that has to be done, and I know is being developed in some places. Additionally, as parents we can be doing it for ourselves. Parenting is a spiritual path, as noble and as near to God as that walked by any monk or nun. Mothers and fathers are the sacred portals through which a human soul is born. We are blessed with a treasured companion, our child, who is alongside both as our guide and as a person we have a responsibility to lead. Children come to teach us new things, just as much as we try to teach them. If you want to be more creative, more playful, more present in the moment and alive to the wonder of the world, you have given life to the best teacher of all these things you will ever have. You will also learn far more about your capacity for anger, fear, laughter, and love.

THE SPIRITUALITY OF THIS BOOK

The sacred is there, in the midst of family life, waiting to be experienced. In this book I offer thirty practical ways in which we can make that discovery. Although I am a practicing Christian of a liberal and progressive kind, this book is spiritual rather than religious. By that I mean that it seeks to work with the natural impulses to search for purpose and meaning that we all have. From our spiritual center comes our deepest voice, our deepest listening, our deepest seeing. We feel ourselves connected to something "other" that is greater than the everyday. It may seem to be an "other" that is out there, transcendent. Or it may be an "other" that is right here, immanent; or it may be both, which is my personal experience. Wherever, it is the place where we feel most fully alive.

We do not have to be religious to be spiritual, but for some it may help. Religion is a collective attempt to understand and facilitate the spiritual experience; it is human made and culture based. Religion is the way we together endeavor to harness the sacred, which is as difficult to seize hold of as a bolt of lightning. Religion is like a metal conductor, grounding the mystery here on earth in spiritual practice, conceptual understanding, personal and social action.

We all ground the mystery in different ways, but there are commonalities that many seem to share. Once you burrow beneath all the customs, myths, rules, language, imagery, and organizations associated with each religious faith, there are broad truths that are agreed upon. Scholars have called it the "perennial philosophy," a term made known by the British writer Aldous Huxley;[1] others call it "universal wisdom" since it can be found across all cultures and throughout the ages. American philosopher Ken Wilber helpfully summarizes it as follows: Spirit exists. Spirit is found within us, but most of us don't realize this because we are living in a world of separation and duality, an illusory state. There is a way out of this illusion, and if we follow this path it leads to enlightenment or a direct experience of spirit. This experience of spirit within leads to happiness, compassion, mercy, and social action on behalf of all sentient beings.[2]

In other words, there is unity and love at the heart of all things, and we are part of that oneness. It can be known to us in our deepest selves, and we have the ability to grow in harmony with it. With that perennial philosophy in mind, this book will help you share with your child:

- A realization of how truly precious we are.
- An appreciation of the wonder of life in all its majesty and mystery.
- A deep sense that there is a unity to all things and that we are all connected to each other and the earth.
- An understanding of the power of love in our lives.
- The ability to use the here and now, imagination, playfulness and creativity as a gateway to the spiritual.

I use the terms "sacred," "the spiritual," and "God" throughout, interchangeably. The latter is the name for the sacred that we are most familiar with in the West; however, you can easily substitute another term that you prefer.

The suggestions I make are often practical, and with the time-pressured reality of our lives in mind, I recommend changes that can be slipped easily into daily life. Many of the suggestions do not come in the form of an addition to your already full "to do" list, but are simply a shift in attitude and awareness about what you are already accomplishing. Raising our children is very much a task grounded in the grittiness of the here and now, and that's exactly the best place for the sacred to be in our lives. Some of the ideas may appeal to you, others not. That is fine. It would be extremely idealistic to think that any family could do all thirty! The concept of the book is that you dip in and out of it and work with those sections that resonate with you and seem right for your children. Your selection is likely to change over time as you and your children journey further along together.

I hope that the thirty ways in this book will appeal to both those who are traditionally religious and those who are exploring the newer forms of spirituality that are emerging. They may be useful for parents who do not share the same religion—an increasingly common situation in our pluralistic society—but are trying to find a mutually acceptable way of nurturing spirituality in their children. The book is intended as an introductory guide for those parents who may have already taken a keen interest in the practical and emotional aspects of child-raising and are now beginning to look out toward the wider horizon.

Caring parents today read many useful parenting books and magazine articles about how to raise children—how to listen to them empathetically, how to build their confidence and self-esteem, how to manage sibling rivalry and gender difference. So far, however, the question of parenting and spirituality remains underexplored. You will find parenting books relating to specific religious traditions, but the broader overarching subject of family spirituality presents a new challenge. I am certainly no guru with all the answers, but I am a seeker committed to having an awareness of the sacred at the heart of my own family life. If you yearn for the same, if you want your family to have more glimpses of the sacred and feel its absence less, try parenting with spirit.

STARTING OUT

Make the Decision to Parent with Spirit

Children are the proof we've been here, they're where we go when we die. They're the best thing and the most impossible thing, but there's nothing else. You have to believe me. Life is a riddle and they are the answer. If there's any answer it has to be them.

ALLISON PEARSON, *I Don't Know How She Does It*

WHAT DOES IT mean to parent with spirit? Is there really an approach to child-rearing that is spiritual? If you are reading this book presumably you believe that there is a spiritual dimension to life, or are at least sympathetic to the idea and do not rule it out entirely. If that is the case then it deserves to have an important place within your family life. To ignore it would be like raising your children in a black and white world, rather than one that you know has the full radiance of color.

There are three facets to the practice, all equally important and interdependent, like a trinity. Let's work through them one at a time.

PARENTING AS A SPIRITUAL PATH

People frequently say that the birth of their child was one of the most memorable moments of their life. My husband and I will never forget the first sight of each of our babies, the first time he or she was cradled in our arms. Even if the labor and delivery was hard and bloody, and I felt I was taken to hell and back, that first witnessing of a child can be a tidal wave of grace that comes to us freely. God is not in some far-off galaxy but here in flesh, a miracle beyond comprehension. Parents often spontaneously weep at how astounding childbirth is. It is also a pivotal experience that sets us off on a new path, the journey of parenthood. Some might feel that it begins even before this landmark day, at discovery of pregnancy. Whichever, we are forever changed by the arrival of the new soul who has been delivered into our care.

As soon as we are immersed in the more mundane day-to-day matters of childcare and work, however, that sense of the extraordinary can soon be lost. The trick is this: make the decision to keep looking for it. View parenthood as an opportunity to grow spiritually. It is not something to be accomplished as soon as possible so that we can get on with our adult life (a moan that many of us have at difficult moments), but an experience to be savored. Parenthood infuses our life with love, the very essence of our spiritual source. It gives us new perceptions of the world: if we crouch alongside our children and look with their eyes, what we see will be wondrous, fun, alive in the moment, and full of possibility.

SPIRITUAL PRACTICE FOR PARENTS

Take quiet time to reflect on and answer these questions:

1. What have been the happiest moments that I have shared with my children?
2. What have been the most difficult challenges that I have faced as a parent?
3. What have I learned from these experiences?

It's lofty to say that God is there during every diaper change, and I would be the first to say that the sacred may seem a million miles away after a long day doing nothing other than react to the obstreperous demands of children, like a ball being bounced around a pinball machine. There will be many times when parenting challenges us to the very core, but it is at such moments that we come to know ourselves better. We will make mistakes, but if we can view these positively as opportunities to learn, we will continue to grow as human beings.

When we become a parent we find ourselves being taught in one of the best monasteries on God's map: it's called the family.

DRAWING UPON A HIGHER POWER

Spiritual parents have a secret resource that they use to help them do their job to the best of their ability. This resource is available to us all, but many of us fail to use it. Like a circuit of electricity that runs through the home, this force only becomes attainable when we make a conscious decision to turn on the power switch at the fuse box. Alcoholics and other addicts make the same conscious decision when they embark on the twelve-step recovery plan, which has had enormous success in treating people whose lives have become unmanageable. I don't want to compare being a parent to being an addict, but when you have children you do sometimes feel that you are losing control of your life and that you need a helping hand. It comes as an enormous relief to discover that help is there and you are not doing the weighty job of raising your children alone. You are in fact coparenting with the source from which we all come, however you understand that creator to be. I have never heard this put more beautifully than in *The Prophet* by Kahlil Gibran:[1]

> You are the bows from which your children as living arrows are
> sent forth.
> The archer sees the mark upon the path of the infinite, and He
> bends you with His might that His arrows may go swift and far.
> Let your bending in the archer's hand be for gladness;
> For even as He loves the arrow that flies, so He loves also the bow
> that is stable.

Use your coparent (God or spirit) to help you when there are difficult decisions to be made, by following your deepest intuition. Trust that this is the best way for you to find the wise outcome that you seek.

From that same spiritual source comes the inspiration and zeal we need to be creative, joyful, and energetic parents. You may suddenly think of an exciting game to play with your children or have a vision of how to spend a perfect Saturday. With enthusiasm, which means "God within," even the routine matters of parenting can be tackled positively and with a sense of fun.

That source is also your wellspring of love, the realm where the most important work of parenting is done. Put aside the educational toy, the worthwhile after-school activity, the children's bedroom makeover, and know for a moment that the crucial things are hugs, kisses, care, compassion, forgiveness, and empathy. Our coparent will help us draw from ourselves these deeper ways of nurturing.

SPIRITUAL PRACTICE FOR PARENTS

Sit quietly and comfortably, go inside yourself and repeat, either aloud or silently, the following mantra: "My God, help me serve my children well. My God, help me serve my children well."

NURTURING YOUR CHILD'S SPIRITUAL DEVELOPMENT

One of our duties as a mother or father is to encourage our children to have a relationship with their spiritual self. You may want to bring up your children within the deepness of a particular faith tradition, or you may prefer to offer something broader and more open. Either way, your family will benefit from being in a home where a spiritual practice is observed.

An Indian proverb says that everyone is like a house with four rooms—physical, mental, emotional, and spiritual. Most of us live mainly in one room, but we need to inhabit them all, daily. The same metaphor can be applied to the family: to be truly holistic all rooms need to be honored. This book will help you find ways to enter your spiritual family room on a regular basis, whether that be through prayer, meditation, story time, family ritual, creativity, or nature. Communicate spiritual ideas to your children when it seems appropriate, and encourage the asking of far-reaching questions. Teach your children to find and value the still, small voice in their head; inspire kindness and let them know that their life has purpose.

Remember, children form their earliest images of God from us. If we are compassionate, loving parents, then God too will be understood as a caring creator.

There is much truth in the old adage that most learning is caught, not taught. How do you live and demonstrate your spirituality? If you believe the world is a joyless, fearful place in which we need to take, take, take rather than give, your children are likely to grow up sharing this view. If we can live in accordance with our spiritual beliefs and be a good role model for our children, the benefits they reap will be enormous. If we treasure our connection to God, our children will learn to treasure their connection too. As Carl Jung puts it, "If there is anything we wish to change in the child, we should first examine it and see whether it is not something that could better be changed in ourselves."

If we want to nurture our children spiritually, we must first nurture ourselves. On an aircraft, parents are always advised to put their oxygen mask on first, before attending to children. How do you get your spiritual oxygen? If you want to parent with spirit, make sure that every day you do those things that you know nourish your own soul. Perhaps you could say a short prayer or have a meditation session (even if it's when washing up!). Or you could take a walk in the park or read a poem at bedtime, or listen to magnificent music in the bath. There are many ways in which we find ourselves close to spirit. You may even find that parenting becomes one of the most spiritually gainful aspects of your life.

SPIRITUAL PRACTICE FOR PARENTS

Take quiet time to reflect on and answer these questions:

1. How do I treasure my connection to spirit?
2. How might I nurture my spiritual self more?
3. What are the ways in which I have already been nurturing the spiritual development of my children?

Recognize Your Child's Natural Spirituality

Our birth is but a sleep and a forgetting:
The Soul that rises with us, our life's Star,
Hath had elsewhere its setting,
And cometh from afar:
Not in entire forgetfulness,
And not in utter nakedness,
But trailing clouds of glory do we come
From God, who is our home:
Heaven lies about us in our infancy!
Shades of the prison-house begin to close
Upon the growing Boy.

WILLIAM WORDSWORTH, *Intimations of Immortality*

PEOPLE OFTEN SAY that when they look into a newborn baby's eyes they get the feeling that there is a wise old soul looking out. This may be an insightful observation, and it raises a tantalizing question. In what spiritual state do our children arrive in the world? Are they empty vessels, waiting for adult spiritual instruction? Do they have only a basic level of spirituality, far inferior to that of a grown-up? Or, as Wordsworth's poem implies, do they come already equipped with something spiritually special? What do you think?

ARE CHILDREN NATURALLY SPIRITUAL?

There is very little academic research to help us with this baffling inquiry. Only a handful of studies have explored the spirituality of children, and many of these have been flawed and covered only a limited sample. As David Hay, the former Director of the Children's Spirituality Project at Nottingham University in the UK explains in *The Spirit of the Child!*[1] (a rare and valuable academic book on this subject) what little research there is has mistakenly focused on language and thought rather than direct spiritual experience. Children, especially young ones, are not able to articulate in words or concepts their experience of God. It may be that only with adult hindsight can we give a childhood spiritual experience verbal expression. Research in the 1970s and '80s from the Religious Experience Research Unit in Oxford noted that a sizeable proportion of the 5,000 accounts it received about spiritual experience were reminiscences of events occurring in childhood, sometimes at a very young age.

David Hay and PhD student Rebecca Nye (coauthor of the above book) worked with children aged six and ten in Nottingham and Birmingham, considering how spirituality (rather than religious teaching) might be given expression. They tried to identify the areas of children's language and behavior where "sparks of spirituality" are found. They then developed a map laying out the geography of what they understood to be children's spiritual experience. This they devised by looking at the converging writings on spirituality and child psychology, and their own research, as well as by putting a finger up to the wind. I find it a very convincing picture. Below is a summary of their three interrelated findings.

Children are "aware"

Being aware of your awareness is of great importance in adult spiritual practice. The ability to be fully present in the moment and focus attention is a discipline that is cultivated in meditation and prayer. Children are exceptionally good at existing in the here and now and not dwelling on the past or contemplating the future. They are also very good at focusing their attention intensely on something that interests them and tuning into the immediacy of an experience. They can be so wrapped up in what they are doing that they become unaware of things going on around them. Daily, children are trying to master new skills such as walking, bicycling, or writing, and they are often able to enter into the joyful flow of these experiences so that their action and awareness merge.

Children are also naturally aware of their bodies. As we grow up we start to ignore this physical sense in favor of cerebral activity.

Children sense mystery

When we sense mystery we become aware that there are unknown aspects of life beyond our everyday existence. In education we spend much of our time trying to understand life in rational bite-sized chunks. A mystical experience can be a shock to the system if you are used to living in this limited way. Wonder and awe are thought to be ways in which we sense the mystery of the sacred. These experiences come very easily to children, who can be mesmerized by something that adults see as mundane, like the striking of a match.

We need imagination to explore mystery, to be able to develop a picture of what is beyond the obvious. If you watch children play you will quickly see that they have highly developed imaginations, and a powerful capacity for and enjoyment of letting go of material reality.

Children sense values

Many people believe that we undervalue feelings in favor of intellect. What is often dismissed as mere emotion is in fact a force that drives us and a measure of what we value. Spirituality is associated with strong feelings: we can be ecstatic when God's presence is felt, and in a black hole of despair when it is felt to be absent. Strong feelings help us grow spiritually, which is probably why many people find faith after a personal crisis. Children are easily in touch with the intense awareness that generates strong feelings of delight and despair.

If they have had good parents, children pick up from a young age the sense that there is ultimate goodness in the world and that they can trust life. If mommy and daddy are kind, then God is too. Children are also often searching for meaning, asking the profound questions that adults can forget to keep asking, like "who am I?" and "why was I born?" This thoughtful expression of spirituality is likely to have grown out of all the previously mentioned signs of a child's spiritual stirring.

Children, then, possibly have a strong connection with that part of being alive that is associated with feelings, and this is certainly an important part of spirituality. But that doesn't mean they are little Buddhas. Ken Wilber, who writes about human consciousness, is more skeptical about children's spiritual capacities. He points out in his book *Integral Psychology* [2] that children are not able to understand the feelings of others; they are self-absorbed and egocentric. They may feel good about being alive, but they haven't yet learned how to empathize and are therefore not able to extend themselves compassionately to others. This is an important part of spirituality, and one that comes only with higher development.

NURTURING A CHILD'S NATURAL SPIRITUALITY

Researchers into children's spirituality suggest that the early experiences that children have of the sacred are soon forgotten as they grow up in the secular world. According to Wordsworth, "shades of the prison house" close in on growing children. This too is how it is viewed in Waldorf education, a spiritually orientated education system founded by Rudolf Steiner. Waldorf educators believe that young children, in order to preserve their spirituality, need to be protected from a premature entry into worldly life. This means keeping the adult modern world of rationality and academics at bay in favor of creative pursuits and traditional handicrafts. Exposure to television and computers is also strongly discouraged. Ken Wilber suggests that it is the higher structures of the mind—the development of the ego, the sense of our self as an individual person, and our conscious mind—which cause this early spiritual potential to be lost.

If children are to maintain the original vision they have of the world, they need to be given a context that allows its expression. This is where parents come in. We can protect the natural spiritual qualities in our children and also provide a structure that will nurture their development into adult life. Think of a young vine: it needs soil, water, and sunlight to keep it alive and ensure growth. It also benefits from a trellis to help it climb and take shape.

AGES AND STAGES

How soon can we start to nurture a child's spirituality? The simple answer is that it's never too soon or too late, but the earlier we start the better. It's important to understand our child's developmental level, otherwise we may have unrealistic expectations. Each stage of a child's development will bring with it different challenges and rewards, and as spiritual parents we need constantly to adapt the spiritual practice within the family to meet changing needs.

BEFORE BIRTH

Spiritual parenting begins as soon as pregnancy, when both mothers and fathers can begin to connect with their growing child through visualizations or prayer. Holding your hands over a swollen pregnant belly and marveling at the miracle happening within is one of life's most sacred experiences. Pregnancy and birth offer an opportunity to open yourself to the absolute wonder of creation. Before I get too sentimental, on the physical level there may of course be nausea, varicose veins, and heartburn; and on the emotional level there may be confusion and fear. However, if your soul was slumped in a secular stupor, pregnancy is a magical wake-up call. Take brief moments whenever you can to experience fully your pregnancy. I always found taking an evening bath an excellent way both to ease tired muscles and retreat and be with my growing baby.

The baby

The most important spiritual message you can give a baby is to let her know that she is loved and safe and can trust the world. Parents and carers need to be close by and attentive, responding quickly to a baby's needs. Talk to and play gently with your baby, cuddle her. Bath with her on your chest: she will love the skin-to-skin contact. Some parents, influenced by a parenting movement called "attachment parenting," believe that it's important to be close to your baby at all times. This includes "wearing" your baby in a sling as often as you can, breast-feeding on demand and sleeping with your baby. This baby-centered approach is thoroughly nurturing, although it has to be countered by the needs of the mother, the parents' relationship, a good night's sleep, and safety issues.

The toddler, 1–2 years

At this stage a child is detaching from the parent for the first time and developing a sense of himself as a person who is separate from the people and world around him. He now starts to explore the world with an enormous curiosity. His interest is not intellectual, but discovery through his senses. What does it look like? How does it feel? How does it taste? An important spiritual gift you can give your child at this stage is to encourage him in his exploration. Be joyful about new accomplishments, like walking. Let your child know that his world is a safe and happy place, and that he is able to cope with new challenges. There will be bumps and knocks, and it's tough as a parent not to overwhelm your child with your own anxiety about the dangers lurking around every corner. Remain calm, take sensible precautions, and remember that your child's experience of pain is his inbuilt safety mechanism, which teaches him where the boundaries lie.

The preschooler

At this stage a child is learning that "I am" becomes "I can." Potty training is just one of many new accomplishments. This is a time when the ego explodes into being in an undisciplined way, resulting in temper tantrums galore. A spiritual gift to offer your child at this time is the reassurance that her feelings are nothing to be frightened about or ashamed of. A toddler can be overwhelmed by her temper outburst and become emotionally flooded. Let her know that she has the ability to come back to her calm center and that she is still loved despite the nightmare scene she caused in the supermarket. The best way you can do this is by remaining calm yourself. Your child may be out of control, but you are not. Keep any teaching you want to share about what's right and wrong very simple: young children's understanding of morality is based primarily on how they feel rewarded or punished. Children at this age become very creative and engage in lots of imaginative play. Do all you can to encourage this. The preschooler will also enjoy listening to simple spiritual stories, and some may be ready to participate in family rituals and short prayers.

Middle childhood 5–8 years

Once children have mastered speech, there are many more sophisticated ways in which you can practice spirituality with them. From now on things can get really interesting! This is the time when your child will start to ask you imponderable questions, like "Does God go to the toilet?" She may also be interested in death, as she struggles to understand our earthly finality. Most children will now be ready to begin to learn simple and short prayer and meditation practices. There are also many spiritual lessons that can be passed on in the form of games, stories, and general fun. These can have an active and creative role in family rituals. This is the time to stress the importance of giving, sharing, and telling the truth, but not through punishment. Encourage your child to be aware that these actions lead to a good feeling inside.

Children this age often like to be outside a lot, using their bodies and experimenting with nature and seeing what it can do. Make plenty of time for outdoor play.

The older child, 8–12 years

Children start to care about events in the world around them at this age—a tragedy on the television news, for example. Ken Wilber says that from seven to eleven there is a profound shift in consciousness, and for the first time children are able to put themselves in someone else's shoes and empathize with another's experience.

Children develop personality and independence at this stage, coming up with their own hobbies and likes and dislikes. The spiritual writer Deepak Chopra believes that a ten-year-old child is capable of wisdom and personal insight. "The child can see and judge through her own eyes; she no longer has to receive the world secondhand from adults," he says.[3] Consequently, this is the time when you may expect some spiritual rebellion. Although this can be disappointing, remember that it is a healthy developmental phase and all part of the journey. It's extremely important from now on to find regular time in which you talk with your children and share in their life, which may increasingly be with their peers and outside the home.

The young teenager, 12–15 years

With adolescence arrives puberty, and needs that parents cannot fulfill. This is a time of letting go and trusting that your child is capable of dealing with life. "The issue is whether the child has an inner self that can be used as a guide," says Deepak Chopra.

From eleven to fifteen a child develops the ability for introspection, and for the first time "Who am I?" becomes a burning issue, according to Ken Wilber. It can be a time of much angst, when teenagers begin to grapple with the truly big questions of life, alongside trying to find their place in the world. Some teenagers can become quite fervent about their spiritual beliefs, others may temporarily forget about them almost entirely.

Do you recognize any of these stages in your own offspring? Children of course all develop at a different pace and the ages cited can be no more than generalizations, but they are useful to help you work out what you might need to be doing to keep those clouds of glory trailing.

SPIRITUAL PRACTICE FOR PARENTS

Take some quiet time to reflect on your own childhood and remember any spiritual experiences you may have had. Were there any times as a child when you felt connected to a larger reality?

Discover Sacred Time in a Busy Life

Now or never! You must live in the present, launch yourself on every wave, find your eternity in each moment.

HENRY DAVID THOREAU

TIME IS A big issue for parents. There simply never seems to be enough of it. The life of a modern mom or dad is a breathless dash to school, to work, to play group, to the supermarket, to ballet lessons, to football practice, to the ironing board, to the sofa (if you're lucky), to bed. I have lost count of the number of Sunday newspapers that remain unread by Monday morning. I have often looked with envy at couples leisurely drinking cappuccino together at the weekends. Sometimes the list of things "to do" that I carry in my head resembles the pile of laundry I have sitting in our utility room: we are talking Mount Everest dimensions.

Javier, a father of two young children, told me that loss of personal time had been the thing he found most difficult about becoming a parent in his forties. Javier, who lives with the Findhorn Foundation, a nondenominational spiritual community in Scotland, had enjoyed space each morning in which he meditated and centered himself for the day ahead. This is now completely impossible with early-rising children to take care of. "All my daily spiritual habits have had to change," he said. "There is so little time for myself now." There is no doubting that when you become a parent you have to make tremendous personal sacrifices and surrender much of the time you might have had for self-nurture. I often think that nuns and monks have got it easy. Their day is punctuated by silence and worship, and they regularly get to go on retreats. Attuning to the transcendent must be a piece of cake in such circumstances. I challenge the most holy Abbot or mountainside yogi to maintain their connection to the sacred after a protracted period with three demanding, screaming, often unreasonable small children in tow. It's a tragic irony of parenthood that never before has your personal time been so eroded, and never before have you needed that "me time" so desperately.

In coming to terms with this dilemma I have found the writing of the Vietnamese Zen master Thich Nhat Hanh helpful. According to this spiritual teacher, we can even wash dishes in a holy way. "While washing the dishes one should only be washing the dishes, which means that while washing the dishes one should be completely aware of the fact that one is washing the dishes," he says. He advises against being sucked into the future while performing this simple act, by dwelling on what nice things we might do when we have finished the task. In so doing we would not be fully alive during the time we are at the sink. "The fact that I am standing there and washing these bowls is a wondrous reality," he says.[1]

This is a demanding teaching to put into practice, but parents to some extent have no choice other than to pray or meditate while on the run, to find our stillness and connection to the divine in brief gasps, like the jogger who rests momentarily to draw breath. Two Buddhist women told me that they used to do their twice daily chanting practice while breast-feeding their babies. For Javier it has meant learning how to find the spiritual in everyday, apparently mundane experiences, like chopping vegetables and sweeping the floor in the Findhorn Foundation kitchen where he works. "This is my challenge at the moment," he says. "This is what interests me." A shift in the kitchen for Javier begins by lighting a candle and gathering with his workmates for an "attunement," in which they share how they are feeling, hold hands and take a moment of silence to connect with the divine.

The shift ends in the same way. It's a ritual that is practiced throughout the Findhorn Foundation when people come together to work. When I stayed with the community I certainly found this discipline a wonderful way of stilling myself so that I could be present in the moment. It also created a very warm team feeling. When my husband John stayed there, he says that even cleaning the toilets became transformed into a sacred experience!

I believe that, as parents, if we can achieve a deeper awareness about life as it is lived and experience our daily activities as part of the larger whole, we will feel much more joyous and balanced when we serve our family. God does not abide only in the heavens: God is here in the middle of our lives, in the laughter of our child, in the sun on our faces, the water pouring from the kitchen tap, the conversation with a neighbor, the chore to be accomplished. What we need to cultivate is the art of tuning our awareness into this spiritual source.

It is in this respect that children can become our spiritual teachers. To them the world is a magical place where commonplace occurrences have the power to transfix them. Whose child has not spent what seems like an eternity playing with water? They pour it, they splash it, they squirt it, and they drink it. To a child, water is a miraculous substance, full of surprises and not to be taken for granted. Add a goldfish to a bowl of the stuff and your child may turn giddy with ecstatic joy. For grown-ups, a fish is rarely a cause for rapture. But in the words of the late comedian George Burns, "You want a miracle? You make a fish from scratch!"

Children give parents an opportunity to revisit the world from a child's perspective. If you haven't already done this, try it for size. It's an exercise in attentiveness and profound delight. I walk through a park on the way to my office in the morning and frequently fail to notice my surroundings because my mind is already racing to the e-mails that await me. In that very same park, and with a child's hand in mine, I am far more inclined to stop, watch squirrels and smell the roses. This has been one of the great gifts of children in my life. And we have it on good authority that it will do us good spiritually: Jesus in the gospel of Matthew said that unless we become like little children we will never enter the Kingdom of Heaven.

Having said that, there is a limit to our regression. We have our adult needs too, and I suspect that most of us have experienced periods of boredom when looking after our children. I have had some of my worst episodes of brain rigor mortis whilst singing "The wheels on the bus go round and round," or posting triangles, circles, and squares into a shape sorter. There comes a time when we need a break and a chance to go off and do grown-up things. For me, working part-time provides me with an invaluable opportunity to use the bits of myself that often seem to wither when I am with my children for sustained periods. Other people may find different solutions. What is important is to become aware of how much you can give whilst still feeling in balance. In the words of David Spangler, father of four, spiritual writer, and former codirector of the Findhorn Foundation, "The soul that lives within each parent is more than just a parent and needs opportunities, just like children, to discover and express other dimensions of personality. Parents are 'selfing' too."[2]

If that adult-only time is as rare to find as an osprey, Thich Nhat Hanh provides yet more wisdom as to how we might embrace the problem. He writes about the father of two who tells him that he has decided not to divide his time into parts anymore. This father tries to consider the time he spends helping his wife or helping his son with homework as his own time too. His own time is no longer just about going for nice walks by himself or reading a book. His own time is everything that he does, so he finds ways of enjoying his family's presence and fully engaging with them. "The remarkable thing is that now I have unlimited time for myself!" he says.

DOWN SHIFTING

"I think the world today is upside down, and is suffering so much, because there is so very little love in the homes and in family life. We have no time for our children, we have no time for each other; there is no time to enjoy each other. Love begins at home," said Mother Teresa. Modern life does move at great speed, and long work hours are a deep-rooted cultural problem. A report by the International Labor Organization says that

Americans work the longest hours in the industrialized world and take the shortest vacations. Over 20 percent say they work close to forty-nine hours a week. If you feel overly hurried, you may need to prioritize so that you have more time available for what is most important. That is easy advice to write, but not so easy to follow, especially if you are burdened with a large mortgage, are a single parent, or have a sense of self-esteem that is bound up with your position on the career ladder. But there can come a time when this challenge has to be tackled. We do have choices in how we use our time. We do not have to be the victims of our busyness. The new phenomenon known as "down shifting" involves a deliberate scaling down of income and lifestyle. Mo, a single parent to her son Ryan, decided to sell her hairdressing business because her work commitments were so onerous she was rarely home before seven in the evening. "I just wasn't seeing Ryan enough," she remembers. "I felt very stressed, and was missing out on his childhood." She is now self-employed and takes in language students as boarders to maintain her income, but says she has no doubts that she has done the right thing. "We are so much happier now. I just needed to have faith that we could make it work."

HOW TO MAKE TIME YOUR FRIEND
RATHER THAN YOUR ENEMY

- Be present in the moment as often as you can, and spiritually savor what you are doing.
- Enjoy the world from your child's perspective, which is often one of wonder and fascination.
- Recognize when you are feeling off-balance and need to restore yourself.
- Explore how your experience of time changes when you don't divide it rigidly into time for others and "me time," but see it all as time for yourself.
- If you can, downshift if you are in need of an uplift: prioritize your life so that you have more time for what matters most.

SPIRITUAL PRACTICE FOR PARENTS

Before you begin a domestic chore, try this brief attunement.

Take a moment to center yourself: you might want to light a
   candle, strike a Tibetan bell or place a meaningful image in
   front of you. All these "devices" help to create a sense of
   the sacred.
Feel yourself present in the moment.
Experience a sense of gratitude for your body and its ability to
   perform this task.
Appreciate the things you are about to work with, whether this
   is water, food, cloth, or heat.
Consider the gift you are offering to others.
Now begin.
Notice whether this attunement helps bring a new awareness
   to a normal domestic task.

Create a
Family Creed

Where there is no vision, the people perish.
Proverbs

W HAT IS THE purpose of your family? Whether you are a
large family, a small family, a single-parent family, a family
with stepchildren or adopted children, why are you all together,
living here on this earth? People the world over, throughout the
ages, have lived in family groups, and no society has ever survived the breakdown of family structures. At a basic level we
need family for reproduction and economic stability; it's also the
most dynamic means we have of turning human beings into
effective citizens. On a soul level, a healthy family is the primary
place in which we experience and practice love, and in so doing
have the opportunity to know God.

We have been divinely designed to live together as partners,
mothers and fathers, daughters and sons, brothers and sisters,
grandparents. We are committed to each other by bonds of affection
and duty. When families go wrong we are profoundly unhappy and
may carry the wounds throughout our lives. However, the impulse
within us to be in family is so strong that we usually risk trying
again. Many of us do our best not to repeat the mistakes that our

own parents made. Most people who have divorced remarry. Some people who find themselves outside of traditional family structures defy the old saying that "blood is thicker than water" by cultivating loving friendships that become as strong as kith and kin. Being in family, whatever its shape or form, is a fundamental need and desire: it is part of God's purpose for us.

In this chapter I am inviting you and your family to press the pause button on your whirl of day-to-day family life, step back, and take a moment together to look at the bigger picture and contemplate your family's spiritual purpose. Ask yourselves: what are we about as a family? What are we for? What sort of family do we want to be? These are fundamental questions that we often fail to ask ourselves because of our busyness of getting on with getting on.

An inspiring way of doing this is by gathering together to create a family creed.

A Family Creed

"Creed" comes from the Latin *credo*, which means "I believe." In Western culture we are most familiar with creeds in a church setting, where they are used as a statement of shared belief or a devotion during which Christians recommit themselves to their faith. Similarly, a family creed is a statement about what you together believe to be the purpose of your family life. You can then use your creed to dedicate yourselves to this end.

It is popular now for organizations to develop a mission statement to inspire people and unify them behind a common cause. Creating a family creed is rather like devising your family's mission statement, and you may prefer to call it a mission or vision statement.

Creating a family creed may prove to be a very powerful experience for you. In his book *The 7 Habits of Highly Effective Families* Stephen R. Covey describes the creation of his family mission statement as the most transforming event in his family history.[1] "Creating a family mission statement has given us a destination and a compass," he writes. I am indebted to Covey for this very valuable book and his many thoughts about how to tackle this process.

Seed your creed

First and foremost, make the creation of your creed a fun experience. Gather the family together somewhere comfortable, provide sweets or chips, and enthuse about what you are about to do.

Keep your meeting short, possibly only five or ten minutes if your children are very young (our first family creed meeting was far too long and ambitious and the children ended up a bit frustrated by the process!).

Provide paper and colored pens and have ready a few useful questions to prompt thought. These, suggested by Covey, are good for older children:

What is the purpose of our family?
What kind of family do we want to be?
What kind of things do we want to do?
What are our highest priorities and goals?
What are our responsibilities?

For younger children I suggest:

What are we like together when we are feeling really kind?
What do you like doing as a family?
If you had three wishes for us as a family, what would they be?

Have a brainstorming session and get everyone to write down their answers to these questions. If the children are too young to write, do it for them. Alternatively, they could draw a picture and talk about it afterward. Don't judge the contributions, but show respect and encouragement.

Knead your creed

It takes time to create a family creed and you may have to meet several times to get to the right wording. Stephen Covey says it took his family about eight months of regular meetings! When creating your creed remember that the process, which can be very bonding, is just as important as the finished result. An adult needs to take your first brainstorming material away and distill the contributions. Are there common themes and suggestions? You may need to supplement the meetings with one-to-one conversations to arrive at the essence of the points made.

Mothers and fathers should separately discuss their contributions if they seem to differ widely.

Try drafting your first family creed and take it back to the table for comment. This is the difficult part: everyone needs to agree on the final result and feel that it represents their views. Try to keep the wording fairly simple so that children can easily say it aloud. As an example, this is our creed:

Our family is a place where we:
Share love;
Respect and listen to each other;
Pray together;
Send kindness into the world;
Have lots of fun!

Stephen Covey has a creed more suited to older children:

The mission of our family is to create a nurturing place of faith, order, truth, love, happiness, and relaxation, and to provide opportunity for each individual to become responsibly independent, and effectively interdependent, in order to serve worthy purposes in society.

Weed your creed

As a living statement of belief and faith, your creed needs to be revisited and revised over time. Even if in essence it stays the same, you may want to change the wording as your children get older. You may want to change some of the principles expressed in the creed as you progress together as a family.

Heed your creed

Now you have got your creed, don't put it away and forget it! Put it up on the wall, somewhere prominent. The children may like to decorate it, or write it out themselves. Keep it alive by referring to it if you have family meetings, or use it as a prayer before you eat a special meal together. It could be referred to at times of trouble or conflict. There may be moments when you need to plead your creed! Everyone should get to learn the family creed by heart so that it can be carried around internally, a bit like the name tag inside a school uniform: when we are out in the world it tells us who we belong to if ever we need to find the way home.

A FAMILY
SPIRITUAL
PRACTICE

Pray with Your Children

When you pray, you open yourself to the influence of the Power which has
revealed itself as Love.

HENRI J.M. NOUWEN

IN THE SAME way that we need oxygen for our bodies to remain
alive, so too do we need a spiritual practice if our soul is to flourish. Life is full of interesting distractions, but without regular
moments of contemplation we may find it difficult to sustain spiritual focus. It is by engaging in a regular prayer or meditation life
that we most powerfully make communion with the transcendent.
According to the great Zen Buddhist teacher Thich Nhat Hanh,
the greatest enemy of the spiritual life is the human tendency to
sleepwalk through life. Prayer calls us to wakefulness.

Prayer is a language, a way of dialoguing with the divine. Like
any language, it has to be learned. In the modern Western world
we are spectacularly failing to teach children the language of
prayer. Few families belong to an organized religion, where once
children might have learned the art of conversing with our creator. And parents cannot expect schools to teach their children
how to pray. Public schools in the United States are required to
maintain a religiously neutral enviroment. In effect this means
that prayer in class is forbidden, although teachers can institute a

"moment of silence." In Britain, schools are required by law to hold a daily collective act of worship, which has proven problematic. Marian Agombar, Chair of the National Association of Standing Advisory Councils for Religious Education, which monitors collective worship in state schools, told me that prayer is difficult to navigate in multicultural schools. Moreover, many teachers themselves are not familiar with prayer and feel uncomfortable with it. "This is a difficult area for schools," she says. "My own personal opinion is that it is the parents' responsibility to teach children how to pray, and while this may be supported by what takes place in school, they should not rely on the school to do it for them." Very few parents today pray at home with their children. I have read (and written) numerous parenting articles for national women's magazines about all manner of important child-rearing strategies, but have yet to see a single one about praying with children.

Let's face it, family prayers are unfashionable, conjuring up nostalgic 1950s images of kneeling children in white cotton nightshirts. "The family that prays together, stays together," went a popular saying of the time. Family prayer seems a charming Christian blast from the past that has no relevance today in a world of Gameboys, cell phones, and *The Simpsons*. People are often incredulous at the suggestion that they could be praying with their children. "Don't I need to belong to an organized religion to do that?" asked one man. "Children aren't interested in doing things like that," said someone else. On both counts, I believe the answer is no.

Prayer is not the preserve of any one religion: all faiths have prayer. It is humankind's most natural and important way of connecting to a larger reality, and it is available to us all. And that includes children. If you are imaginative in the way that you approach prayer with your children, they really enjoy it. A shared prayer can be the most intimate and meaningful part of your family day. Your child will love the fact that he or she has your full attention, and that you feel cozy together and bathed in love. And for those few minutes the dynamic of your relationship changes—from parent and child to soul mates. My seven-year-old son Benedict has particularly taken to bedtime prayer, and always asks for it should I try to leave his bedroom hastily to get on with my chores.

The title of this chapter is "Pray with Your Children." It is not enough to hand your child some written prayers and tell her to get on with it. Would you hand a five-year-old a piano and sheet music and tell him to play? While children are still young, a parent needs to be alongside them, praying with them. And that, of course, means that you have to know how to pray yourself. It may be that you already pray regularly, or it may be that you did so as a child and have now grown "rusty." I know that some of today's parents might have been forced into inappropriate adult-style prayer when they were young and now feel that the experience holds no benefit for them or their children. I urge them to look again. Or it may be that you have never attempted anything more than invoking God's name when expressing relief, surprise, or anger.

You now have a very good reason to begin to pray. Children bring so many gifts into our lives, including the motivation to do things for them that we might not have done just for ourselves. There is no shame in learning how to pray together. You may find that your child ends up being your perfect teacher.

WHY PRAYER NURTURES A FAMILY'S SPIRIT

- *Prayer helps children feel connected to a larger reality.* Prayer is an expansion of the consciousness and a suspension of ordinary thought. In some ways, prayer is a small act, as easy as reaching out and flicking on a light switch. However, once that light is shining, everything appears differently. You are seeing life as it truly is, albeit briefly. In praying with your children, you are showing them how simple it is to press the switch: to close their eyes, go inside, and "turn on" an experience of a larger reality.

- *Prayer promotes the development of an interior life.* In prayer we quiet the hubbub of the day and hear a deeper part of ourselves instead. Children, just as adults, have an inner life, a world of thoughts and feelings. In prayer, they begin to learn how to attend to these emotions, to sort through them, understand them, and possibly change them. Prayer teaches children self-awareness.

- *Prayer encourages an examination of conscience.* In prayer, we allow God to enter into the center of our person. In so doing we shine a light on the dark corners, where we might otherwise have preferred not to have looked. Ask your children when they pray to go through the day's events, and gently ask them whether there is anything they have said or done about which they feel bad. This is not about berating your children, but a chance for them to offer these things up to God, say sorry, ask for forgiveness, and feel reconciled. It's important to let your children know they are still loved despite their misbehavior.

- *Prayer acts as a tool for transformation.* Prayer is an act filled with hope. We pray in faith that things can be better, that the world may become a happier place, and that we may fulfill our own human potential. In so doing, we accept that we currently have limitations, but we invite God to help us overcome these. In prayer children put their energy and commitment into positive change.

- *Prayer develops gratitude and joy.* In prayer we count our blessings. Encourage your children to think about all the good things that they have in their lives, and to thank God for them. Big and small things can be included in their thanks. They may want to thank God for family and friends, pets, toys, outings, even TV programs they have enjoyed. Prayers of gratitude help children appreciate their world and the people in it, and cultivate an attitude of joy. They also counter feelings of greed.

- *Prayer increases children's engagement in the world.* We can use our prayer to contemplate the wider world and set our lives into a bigger perspective. Encourage your children to think of people who are sick or lonely or experiencing personal problems. Think too of people in other countries who might be suffering from poverty, famine, or war. Your children may want to pray for animals and the earth. Older children may alight on causes about which they feel strongly. Prayer promotes compassion.

- *Prayer brings parents and children together.* Praying with your children can be an extremely intimate moment.

This is especially true if you are speaking aloud spontaneous prayers. On one level this type of prayer is a profound sharing of thoughts and feelings. In joining each
other in this, we overcome our sense of isolation.
Children feel tremendously valued and cared for when
you say prayers that ask God to help them in their personal struggles.

♦ *Prayer develops reverence for the world.* In prayer we take a
moment to value the world God has made. We contemplate the wonder and majesty of creation and honor the
presence of the sacred. Reverence helps nurture respectful behavior in children.

♦ *Prayer helps children feel safe at night.* Prayer is a comfort-
ing ritual that prepares children for sleep. It is an opportunity to let go of cares and worries from the day, to feel
safe and loved. Bedtime is a perfect moment to pray since
it acts as a bridge between the day and the unconscious-
ness of sleep.

♦ *Prayer encourages positive behavior.* Loving and compassionate thoughts will ultimately translate into loving and
compassionate behavior. Children will be more mindful
about their actions and aware that they should be behaving in a way that is acceptable to God.

And, finally . . .

♦ *Prayer may have a mysterious power all of its own.* You may
find it easy to believe that prayer changes something within the person who is praying. But prayer traditionally has
another function too: it is thought to change the world
beyond ourselves. How can this be? Is there any real
sense in which God is able to respond to our pleas for
help? How can you and your children praying for people
you have never met, in a far-off country you may never
have been to, really make a difference? How can prayer
alter the path of a disease? Or protect people from a natural disaster? This is a big question, which stands at the fore-
front of theological debate. I go further into this in the next

chapter. The latest developments in physics can explain a way in which prayer for others might work. Whether you believe it is a matter of personal faith.

AT WHAT AGE?

The earlier you can begin to pray with your children, the better. Younger children are likely to be far more willing to participate than the over-tens. I started to share simple, short prayers with my children when they were about two-and-a-half and had sufficient vocabulary to join in. They also need to be able to remain still for a few minutes. Introducing prayer to older children may be more difficult because they are likely to see it as "uncool" and feel anxious if none of their friends are doing it. Older children may be becoming more rebellious too, which won't help matters. However, if you are fortunate enough to have an older child who is open to the experience, prayer at this age can be more sophisticated and developed. Make prayer a daily habit within your family, so that it is seen to be something as ordinary as a book at bedtime and cleaning teeth.

HOW TO PRAY WITH YOUR CHILDREN

Absolutely everything we do in life can be seen as a prayer, if it is done mindfully, with the intention of bringing ourselves closer to God. Dancing, playing a musical instrument, drawing, cooking, running, even sex and washing the floor can all be prayerful activities. Living your whole life as a prayer would be very wonderful indeed, but few of us are capable of sustaining such a focus on the divine. For this reason formal prayers are a very useful discipline. These too can be many and varied. This is good news, for you may need to introduce different styles of prayer to your children to keep the experience alive and escape empty routine. Don't feel restrained by notions of how prayer should be done: God is not only to be found when we are on our knees with our hands together. Be creative in the ways in which you pray with your children. If children are having fun and participating in prayer that they find stimulating they are much more likely to want to make it part of their life. Here are different kinds of prayers to try with your children.

Spontaneous prayers

These are prayers that are spoken in the moment, from the heart. Your children may want to thank God for things in their life, ask God for help, say sorry for things they have said and done that they feel bad about. Spontaneous prayers can be spoken by both parent and child, either taking it in turns or as it comes. Let the spirit move you!

Prayers from books

There are some captivating anthologies of children's prayers on the market, and I have included a few of my favorites at the end of this chapter. On some nights it may be enough simply to read slowly one of these. Older children may wish to read the prayer themselves.

Memorized prayers

In time children may learn a written prayer by heart. This means just what it says, by heart. Once your child has memorized a prayer, the best place for it to take up residence is in the heart, as a feeling, not in the head just as words.

Prayers with movement

Children respond very well to using movement when they pray. Who says prayers have to be quiet and solemn? Children can jump up and down to express their joy and gratitude for the world. Some written prayers adapt well to the use of hand gestures for illustration. For example, see the "Sarum Primer" in the short anthology at the end of this chapter.

"Creative" prayers

Children may like to write down their prayers and post them into a prayer box that you have made specifically for the purpose. Alternatively you could borrow an idea from Tibetan Buddhists, who fly prayer flags. These are in a variety of symbolic colors, which represent the five elements. Create your own flags, from fabric or tissue paper, and write blessings for the world on them. String them from a tree in your yard.

Silent prayers

When children have reached a sufficient level of maturity in prayer, a period of silent prayer may draw them deeper into the life of spirit. Some people view silent prayer as the most effective way of reaching God, and silence is highly revered by all religions. Quakers for instance base their worship on shared silence. Keep the period of silence fairly short—you will easily be able to notice when your child starts to become restless. An object to focus on may help your child's contemplation—a candle, an object from nature, or a photograph of a nature scene. You may want to introduce a period of silence into some of the other styles of praying mentioned here. When it's effective, a silent prayer is an extremely intimate moment with God.

Prayers with objects

Having a devotional object to hold can help children focus their wandering attention. Children also find it a lot of fun. Prayer beads have been used by most faiths as an instrument of prayer, notably the Catholic rosary. Beads are often used as a way of counting simple repeated mantras or prayers. You could make prayer bracelets or necklaces of your own and use them when repeating a short phrase.

Another idea is to create a cairn—a pile of stones used as a marker to show walkers the way in remote countryside. This works best when there are a number of you gathered for a communal prayer. In turn, place your pebbles into a pile in the center, and as you do so speak aloud your prayers.

This is an engaging way of helping children take stock of their day or week. Collect three stones: one a smooth pebble, one a jagged piece of flint, and the third a sparkling gem. Offer the children each of the three stones. As they hold the pebble encourage them to recollect an ordinary moment of the day for which they feel grateful. With the flint, they recollect a moment that was difficult for them. And with the gemstone they recollect a moment that was sparkly and happy.

WHERE AND WHEN?

Prayers can be said at any time of the day. Although I advocate bedtime prayer in this chapter, mornings are another traditional time for worship. The dawning of a new day seems an appropriate moment to give thanks for new beginnings and consider the challenges ahead. In the whirl of a school run a brief prayer may help everyone fleetingly touch base. When my children are all assembled at the front door in their coats and shoes, clutching lunchboxes and book bags, we occasionally take a few seconds (literally) to hold hands and say a brief prayer. It really doesn't take much at all or make us any later than we might already be. But it's a powerful moment, one that really gathers us together and seems miraculously to create a breath of calm amidst the yelling and frayed tempers that usually characterize our morning departures.

We say bedtime prayers in the children's bedrooms. My younger two children share a room, and we usually pray together while they are lying in bed. My eldest very much enjoys saying prayers without his siblings present. He is usually lying in bed too, and we hold hands. Sometimes we gather together in the living room for a whole-family prayer, sitting in a circle on the floor around a candle. If you have created a home altar (see chapter 20), this may be the perfect spot for it. There really are no rules about this. Try it, and see what works for your family.

PRAYER TROUBLESHOOTING

It would be idealistic to expect family prayer always to go according to your plans. You are not praying with a group of hushed and reverential nuns or monks. That would be easy! The family cloister is anything but peaceful, so expect some chaos. Fights may break out between siblings, battery-operated toys may suddenly come to life, someone may dash out of the room for a pee, conversations may start that have nothing to do with the task in hand. There may be giggles, moans, and yawns. You may want your children to pray like angels for peace on earth, and instead they start demanding that God give them the latest action-hero toy they saw on TV, or that someone they dislike at school suffers some misadventure. All this is normal, and if you expect anything else you will only be setting yourself up for enormous disappointment. In other words, don't hope for heavenly choirs and radiant bursts of light. There will be times when your achievements may seem very modest indeed, and then suddenly your children will say something in prayer that takes your breath away. Appreciate the triumphs when they do come, which they will, for prayer inevitably works its own magic.

Watch out for:

- *Using prayer to manipulate your children.* Be careful not to use prayer as a way of coercing children to behave in the way you would like them to. They will soon pick up on this manipulation.
- *Glossing over problems with prayer.* You may ask for God's help when there are family conflicts and problems, but this doesn't replace the need to discuss difficult issues and work through them.
- *Making children perform.* Don't put children on the spot by expecting them to recite perfect prayers as in a performance.
- *Inappropriate prayers.* Children are occasionally bound to pray selfishly for toys and candy. They may even wish for bad things to happen to people they feel angry with. Avoid chastising them, because they may then associate the whole prayer experience with being told off. Try to steer your children toward prayers of gratitude for what they already have, and suggest that they think of a kinder prayer to replace their vengeful one.
- *Prayers becoming boring.* Like anything else in life that you do frequently, prayer can become routine and dull. Run through the range of possible variations, possibly by praying in different ways on different nights. Buy new prayer anthologies for inspiration. Keep abreast of your

children as they develop: a more sophisticated approach may be needed.

WHEN A CHILD DOESN'T WANT TO PRAY

It may be frustrating and disappointing, but there are likely to be times when your children don't want to pray. You may think of it as a life essential, they think it's "boring and a waste of time." You may think of it as a meaningful way to connect and be together, they think it's intrusive. What's going wrong?

It's worth asking yourself whether you are falling into some of the possible traps associated with praying alongside children (see above).

If you are sure this is not the case, all you can ultimately do is remain positive and patient, and persevere. If you try to discipline your children into praying you are likely to make them even more resistant. Ask them why they don't want to pray. Would they like to do it differently? Perhaps they would prefer to pray alone?[1] Rebelling against prayer and the spiritual life is likely to be a healthy and normal part of growing up. Your children may return to prayer at a later stage. Like riding a bike, once they have learned how, they will never forget. And you can pray for them and continue to point the way. As Thich Nhat Hanh says, "If one person in a family is mindful, all the others will become mindful."

A "TASTER" ANTHOLOGY OF PRAYERS

Guardian angel, protect me today,
Watch over me while I work and play.
Let me be kind and loving and good,
Help me to do the things I should.
    Anonymous, *Circle of Grace*

God watches over us all the day,
At home, at school, and at our play,
And when the sun has left the skies,
He watches with a million eyes.
    Gabriel Setoun, *Circle of Grace*

God be in my head, and in my understanding;
God be in my eyes, and in my looking;
God be in my mouth, and in my speaking;
God be in my heart, and in my thinking;
God be at my end, and in my departing.
Sarum Primer, fifteenth century

Bless my hair and bless my toes
Bless my ears and bless my nose
Bless my eyes and bless each hand
Bless the feet on which I stand
Bless my elbows, bless each knee:
God bless every part of me.
Lois Rock [2]

Daylight always follows night, darkness takes its turn with light,
Darkness is where all dreams begin,
As around the sun we spin.
Diane Baker [3]

Like a tree that grows tall and stately,
Father God . . . Help us grow closer to you.
Like a field of crops growing thick and golden,
Father God . . . Help us grow closer to you.
Like a flower growing toward the sun,
Father God . . . Help us grow closer to you.
Like fruit growing ripe and rosy,
Father God . . . Help us grow closer to you.
Anonymous. [4]

I see the moon,
And the moon sees me:
God bless the moon,
And God bless me.
Traditional

6

Practice Parents' Prayer

The power of prayer is very clear in the profound way that my times of meditation and contemplation have, in fact, changed me. They have helped me to face more honestly who I am and how I impact others.

JOHN SHELBY SPONG, *in A New Christianity for a New World*

WE ALL KNOW that priceless moment when we steal into our children's rooms at night to sneak a peak at their angelic faces on the pillow. If you are feeling angry or resentful after a fractious day as a parent, it all melts away when you see them asleep. In that moment I always recognize how beautiful they are and how much I love them. I see something of their soul nature as they lie there in their unconscious world, motionless, as if suspended in time. What is it about witnessing our sleeping children that is able to transform difficult feelings and generate such a spontaneous outpouring of love? I think the experience is like a natural prayer, albeit unconscious: we contemplate our children and in so doing see their essential goodness. We step outside of the everyday, and take a long, slow look at what is important. To have a spiritual experience the heart needs to be softened and tenderized. There is a popular metaphor that says that the heart needs to be hatched. Gazing at our dreaming children is a very effective incubator.

You may never have sat down and prayed for your children, but if you are familiar with the experience described above, it simply involves taking one more step: becoming consciously aware of what is happening. You have entered into a relationship with God, the eternal Spirit and source of love. As in other relationships you have with those who are close to you, you can have a conversation together. This involves both talking and listening.

You may want to give God thanks for your children, or ask God to help them with a particular struggle they are facing. You may also want to ask God to help you deal with an aspect of parenthood that is perplexing you. You might ask questions and listen for answers.

This is advice that is seldom disseminated in our secular culture. We are told how important it is to make time for ourselves, to telephone a friend or take a few deep breaths when the going gets tough. The huge benefits to be found in stopping for a short while to say a prayer are overlooked, but the bottom line is that praying for our children and ourselves as parents will make us better mothers and fathers.

Praying for our children feeds our love for them. It's like shoveling a heap of coal onto the flame of affection we feel. Praying for ourselves as parents heals the bits of ourselves that may be angry, exhausted, exasperated, anxious. If we listen to that still voice inside us we will be given insights into family struggles and hear suggestions about ways forward. Prayer nurtures our compassion toward our children, which in turn makes us more sympathetic to their problems. In prayer we may be able to find a way through to forgive a child who has been behaving badly.

Prayer is not a magic wand, but it does help. For example, I was feeling at the end of my tether with my eldest son's persistent aggression toward his younger brother. I was even beginning to dislike him and could feel my teeth clenching and fists tightening whenever I was dealing with one of his sibling attacks. On bad days I really wanted to smack him, and did on a couple of occasions. Not because I thought that it would be a productive form of punishment (it's hardly a good way of teaching a child that it's wrong to hit his brother), but because I was brimming with rage and frustration. Eventually, during a desperate moment, I sat down and said a prayer. Within a few seconds everything I felt changed. I asked God to help me to remain calmer and more loving toward my son. And I did. I asked God to help my son overcome the angry feelings he had. And it was then, with great tenderness, that I realized how much our son needed to be loved and held, and to know that his place in our hearts was secure, no matter how many other siblings came along trying to steal the show. The rest of the day was much happier for everyone because I took that brief moment of prayer. The sibling rivalry hasn't completely disappeared of course, but prayer does seem to nudge us all along in the right direction.

WILL GOD HELP OUR CHILDREN IF WE ASK?

Even those skeptical about prayer will concede that it's a useful psychological tool that can result in positive personal change. But can it go yet further? Does prayer help the person for whom we are praying? For example, will a sick child get better because someone is pleading her cause to God? Throughout the centuries, the devout have gathered together to offer petitionary prayer in the belief that God will hear their requests and act on their behalf. Is this the way the universe works? That's a heavyweight issue being hotly debated by theologians and scientists. For many, this type of God died in the eighteenth century as a result of scientific advances. There is no room for God in an objective world of measurable cause and effect. At best, God may have created it all and set the laws of nature in motion, but he doesn't have the power to intervene and answer prayers. If he did, why does he answer some prayers and not others? What sort of God would do that? I am currently vexed by this theological issue possibly more than any other, and at this stage of my journey will say that I do not know whether I believe in the effectiveness of this type of petitionary prayer. I do know, however, that it naturally feels right to me that I should ask God to help me, my children, and other people in the world. Just as God requests me to do his will, so I can make requests of God. In so doing I hope I am creating a positive energy in the world.

Here are some ideas that may help us see a way into this mystery.

Scientific studies of prayer

There is a small amount of scientific research that seems to indicate that prayer might work. One study published in the *Journal of Reproductive Medicine* followed nearly 200 women in South Korea on an IVF program. Unbeknown to them, half of the women were being prayed for by Christians in North America and Australia, who had their photographs. The results were surprising, particularly for the researchers who had intended to prove that prayer doesn't work. The women being prayed for had a 50 percent success rate, compared with a 26 percent success rate for those not prayed for.

Another study, published in *The American Heart Journal*, covered 150 cardiac patients. They had been divided into five groups: one group received just standard care and the others additionally received guided imagery, stress relaxation, healing touch or intercessory prayer (by seven religious groups around the world, including Buddhists in Nepal, Carmelite nuns in the U.S., and a group that grants e-mail requests for prayers to be written down and placed at the Wailing Wall in Jerusalem). It was discovered that, after allowing for all manner of variables, those who received the additional "therapies" showed a 25 to 30 percent better recovery rate, and the group being prayed for fared the best, with a 50 to 100 percent better recovery rate.

New science and prayer

Those of us brought up in the modern age of science, not swayed by faith alone, need to understand the mechanism by which petitionary prayer is possible if we are to find it convincing. The new science of quantum physics may point toward an explanation. In quantum physics matter is studied at its most fundamental level, the subatomic. It has been an exploration full of surprises and mysteries, and seems to break all the rules of established classical physics. Experiments have shown that if two subatomic particles that have been in contact are separated, a change in one is instantly correlated with an identical change in the other. If one is set spinning, its twin also spins. The distance they are apart seems to have no bearing on this interaction. At the moment no one can explain how these so called "nonlocal" events take place. There is no travel time or any known form of energy flowing between the particles, and they cannot be shielded from each other. One hypothesis is that there may be a realm of reality that goes beyond the physical where the subatomic particles are able to influence each other from a distance. Could it be that this is the same realm of reality that allows human consciousness, through petitionary prayer, to have an impact elsewhere? It may be that our consciousness is not confined to our head, nor fixed in time, just as a subatomic particle seems to have a life that can stretch beyond its immediate locality.

Furthermore, quantum physics shows us that the material world is not as material as we think, and that the deeper we look into the substance of the universe the established Newtonian laws of cause and effect don't hold true. Crucially, it was found that particles can also be waves, depending on how we look at them. If we look at them in one way, they are particles; if we look at them in another way, they are waves. The wave form also shows an ability to be in two places at the same time, something that is impossible according to the known laws of physics. "At the quantum level nothing of the material world is left intact," writes Deepak Chopra in his book *How to Know God*.[1] When you hold up your hand, he says, it is strange to realize "that it is actually, at a deeper level, invisible vibrations taking place in a void." To me petitionary prayer does not seem to be such an impossibility in a world such as this.

PARENTAL BLESSINGS

A blessing is a special type of prayer in which you send loving energy to a person, animal, place, or object. Giving your child a blessing is a powerful experience for both you and the recipient. You don't have to be a priest or designated holy person to give a blessing, you just need to have a genuine desire to extend your love and care to someone else. You also need the ability to imagine yourself as a channel of love and goodness, which flows through you and is absorbed by your child.

To give your child a blessing, first center yourself by thinking calming thoughts. You might want to imagine your feet rooted into the ground and your body embraced by the gentle sun. This type of imagery seems to work for many people. Think lovingly and kindly about your child, and allow these feelings to radiate from your heart. Now imagine that this loving energy is moving from your heart, down your arms, and through your hands. Hold your hands, palms down, over your child, and let these vibrations of love and goodness pass into your child. There may be a simple blessing that you'd like to recite, like this one that comes from the Sufi tradition: "Peace to you from my heart to your heart." Or you may prefer silence.

You can give a parental blessing with an awake and willing child, or when your child is asleep. It may be a practice that you find helpful if your child is experiencing a particular difficulty, or as a farewell if you are about to be parted from each other for a period of time.

SPIRITUAL PRACTICE FOR PARENTS

Soften your heart by sitting at the bedside of your sleeping child and slowly taking in deeply every detail that you see. Look at her hair, her eyelashes, the quiver of an eyelid, the smallness of hands and fingers. Watch for her breath, listen for any murmur, watch for any stir. Notice what warm feelings are aroused in you and encourage their growth.

What would you like to say to your child? Imagine that this is a miraculous moment in which you can whisper words that will be taken deep into her soul and guide her in life. Lean forward and whisper those words into her ear . . .

A PARENTS' PRAYER

Let me still myself,
Open my hands to you,
Surrender to you the merry-go-round of thoughts,
And tasks of my life as a parent.

Let me still myself,
Open my arms to you,
And rejoice with you at the gift of the beautiful child,
Who came from you, through me.
Let me still myself,
Open my heart to you,
Ask that you warm its cold, bruised, dark places,
So that I may shine love upon my child.

Let me still myself,
Bow down in your honor,
And as we part entrust to your keeping,
The precious child whose face I hold before you.

Meditate with Your Children

It is only through meditation that you can undertake the journey to discover your true nature, and so find the stability and confidence you will need to live, and die well. Meditation is the road to enlightenment.

SOGYAL RINPOCHE, *The Tibetan Book of Living and Dying*

THEY DON'T APPEAR to go together, do they, children and meditation? Wriggly, jumpy, squeaky, giggly children seem the most unlikely candidates for sitting quietly in the lotus position and calming their mind. You might think that you would have more success teaching a jellyfish how to still itself for five minutes than a child. Not so, however, according to educators in the East, who have a long tradition of successfully teaching the practice to children. Meditation is taught widely to adults in Western culture, often through Buddhist groups, but the idea that children can learn the art too is relatively new, radical even. Proponents of children's meditation claim the benefits are many, and are urgently needed by modern children who often lack any sort of inner life because of the machine-gun rapidity of their world.

Meditation is the life force of all spiritual traditions and one of the most significant ways in which we can transcend daily life and connect to our inner selves. It is an ancient practice, dating back to at least 1500 BC and the authors of the Hindu Vedas. In meditation you learn how to still the chatter of the conscious mind and for a while put to rest all those grocery lists, decorating plans, unpaid bills, and conversations with colleagues, and focus instead on a single, simple experience, often the sensation of breath in your nostrils. It is a training of our attention, in which the mind is watchful and alert, peaceful and detached from the incessant babble that typically hijacks our heads. "Your mind can be thought of as a pond. Thoughts are like rainstorms ruffling the surface of the water and meditation is a way of letting the ripples subside until you have a clear, smooth, reflective pool once more," says Caroline Mann, a learning consultant who has written a PhD on children and meditation.[1]

Meditation isn't easy: people can practice it for years and feel they have got nowhere. It doesn't suit everyone, although often it is those who find it very perplexing who need it most. Those "to do" lists have a nasty habit of repeatedly creeping back into your awareness. Meditation teachers advise that you notice them and gently let them pass by while maintaining your focus. When meditation goes well, many benefits are experienced. Generally the advantages meditation provides to adults can also be experienced by children of three to five years and older, although the practice does have to be modified to cater for their particular needs. I met Carolina, the ten-year-old daughter of a woman who became a Buddhist nun after she was born. She has grown up, since the age of three, in and around a Buddhist community and has been meditating throughout this time. "I think it makes me happier and more patient," she told me. "At the moment I prefer meditating in a group rather than on my own. I find it easier that way." Her mother, Kelshang Shraddha, is involved in running a kids group at the Bodhisattva Buddhist Center in the UK, which teaches children simple meditation practices each Sunday morning. "We try to make it fun and not at all heavy," she explains. "We don't push the children to meditate: some come in very able and focused, others less so. They respond well to those meditations that help them create a positive attitude and work on their feelings. I think the breathing meditations are more difficult with children, as they are pretty abstract. It isn't necessarily always the oldest children who are the best at it: I've seen three-year-olds more concentrated than ten-year-olds. I like to think that when we teach children meditation we are leaving imprints. It is a positive experience that they will later remember as a happy moment."

There are signs that schools in the U.S. are becoming interested in teaching meditation. The Committee to Promote Transcendental Meditation in Schools is urging Chicago-area public and private school educators to consider adding twenty minutes of daily Transcendental Meditation to their curriculums, saying the technique reduces stress, rejuvenates the body and mind, and improves academic performance. So far, Transcendental Meditation programs have been incorporated into three schools in Iowa, Washington, D.C., and Michigan. Caroline Mann, who lectures to teachers and principals about meditating with children in the UK, says that increasingly she is being asked to speak on the subject. "Meditation trains the mind to focus and concentrate. It brings the mind to a point of relaxed, alert attention to the present moment. It is in this state of mental presence that learning is at its most effective and most effortless. It also has a profound effect on self-discipline and behavior," she explains.

WHY MEDITATION NURTURES A FAMILY'S SPIRIT

Psychologists David Fontana and Ingrid Slack have considerable experience of teaching children meditation and have written an excellent book on the subject, *Teaching Meditation to Children*.[2] Here are the ways in which they believe meditation can help us.

- ✦ *Meditation encourages physical relaxation.* During meditation we tune into our body and are able to identify areas of tension and then relax them.
- ✦ *Meditation improves concentration.* Meditation depends on concentration and is one of the best ways of developing it.
- ✦ *Meditation helps us control our thought processes.* In meditation we learn how to be aware of our thoughts, observe them, and let them pass without being sidetracked by them. Unwelcome thoughts can have less power over the mind.

❧ *Meditation increases tranquility and our ability to deal with stress.* As with thoughts, emotions can dominate the mind. In meditation we learn how to be aware of anger or sadness and to experience inner peace in spite of them.

❧ *Meditation improves mindfulness.* Mindfulness is the ability to be aware of what we are experiencing, as we experience it. It's being fully awake to the moment, which in itself is the art of meditation.

❧ *Meditation enhances self-understanding.* In meditation we become aware of the piece of ourselves that lies beyond the conscious mind.

❧ *Meditation improves creative thinking.* If we can open up the unconscious levels of the mind, we have access to all the original ideas that are born there.

❧ *Meditation improves memory.* Much of our forgetting is caused by a failure to concentrate. All-consuming emotions also cause us to forget things. Meditation helps us to be fully aware of what it is we need to remember.

❧ *Meditation enhances spiritual development.* In meditation we can experience the interconnectedness of the world, and compassion and love for everyone and everything around us.

It's a long and impressive list, which may seem idealistic given the boisterous child you have before you. Fontana and Slack do stress that you shouldn't expect too much, and remember that young children have a short attention span. You are planting seeds, which may only visibly germinate later. Some children will surprise you and prove to be very accomplished at meditating. Never show disappointment or impatience with your child; keep the experience relaxed and fun and offer meditation rather than force them into it. If after a couple of sessions they are obviously resistant and not enjoying themselves, leave it until they are older.

HOW, WHEN, AND WHERE?

Presumably, you would only be interested in teaching your children to meditate if you do it yourself and are aware of the benefits. The children's meditation teachers I have spoken to recommend that you should be practicing meditation yourself if you are to teach your young ones how to do it. So how old do children need to be? Caroline Mann thinks that seven is a good age to start, but guided visualization, which is related to meditation (see chapter 15), can be used from as young as three or four. "The earlier you get them to do it, the better. It becomes natural, not something spooky or different. It's just another thing like brushing your teeth," she says. Fontana and Slack recommend starting as early as five, with short one-minute sessions.

Choose a regular time in which to meditate with your child: they like routine. Before bedtime may work well, as long as they are not too tired. Give some thought to the environment in which you do it. This may be a wonderful opportunity to use your home altar if you have one (see chapter 20). "Go to a particular place, and light a candle. It's helpful to have a ritual around it as a subliminal message to the brain to prepare you," says Mann. Low lighting and soft music help create a conducive atmosphere: New Age-type soothing sounds of water trickling and birds singing are ideal.

It's a myth that meditation has to be practiced in the lotus position (cross-legged, with the feet resting on the inside of the opposite thigh). You can sit, kneel, stand, or even lie down, although you are more inclined to fall asleep in the latter position. Teachers generally recommend that the back is straight, head upright, and eyes looking slightly downward. Eyes should be closed to start with to avoid distractions. Children tend to be very able at sitting cross-legged, so this is a suitable position to encourage, with hands lightly folded in the lap.

You may find it helpful to engage in a short burst of physical activity before you start. Together, stretch up on your toes trying to reach the sky, then shake your hands, legs, and body, and even make a few energy-releasing noises, if the neighbors can stand it. You are now ready to begin.

MEDITATIONS TO TRY

There are many different meditations that are suitable for children. The two important and basic practices described here make an excellent starting place.

Meditation focusing on the breath

In a gentle voice, guide your child through this meditation at a relaxed pace. A minute or two is enough for a beginner, building up to ten minutes or so, depending on ability.

Be aware of your breathing, the feeling of air as it enters your nose and is then breathed out. What does it feel like? Is it cool in your nostrils as you take it in, and then warm as you breathe it out? Focus on this sensation. Where do you first feel the air as it touches your nose? If any other thoughts enter your head, let them pass by, without taking notice, like clouds being blown across the sky. Keep focusing on your breath, gently in and out. You can then encourage your child to count while she breathes, which will help her to focus on the breath, blocking out distractions. Ask her to count "one" on the first in-breath, then "one" again on the out-breath, "two" on the next in-breath and so on, up to ten. At ten she should start again at one, and if she loses track, also go back to one.

Meditation for loving kindness

This meditation, which is a traditional Buddhist practice, nurtures unselfish love and kindness in children. You should start with focusing on the breath, as described at the beginning of the previous meditation. Then guide your child through the following visualization.

As you breathe in and out, become aware of yourself sitting here in this room. You are a wonderful child, and you love yourself just as you are. Feel love and acceptance for yourself. Imagine yourself bathed in the warm glow of this love. You are now going to give some of this love to the people who are closest to you. It might be your mommy and daddy, brothers and sisters, grandparents. Let love flow between you. You might want to imagine that you are hugging each other. Now extend this hug to include some of your best friends. Feel your love and warmth for them. Now think about people you know less well. It may be the man in the corner shop, someone you see on the way to school, a pupil you've never spoken to. Let this feeling of love and warmth extend to the people you are feeling angry with, the people you don't much like right now. Include them too in the warm flow of this love. Experience how nice it is too feel good about them. Now go further and allow your love to reach out to people you have never met, children and grown-ups in other countries, particularly those who are short of food and money, those who are sick or in countries at war. Extend your love yet further, to the flowers and trees, animals, rivers, and mountains, and faraway stars. Your love is vast. You are love.

Create Home Rituals

The function of ritual as I understand it, is to give form to human life, not in the way of mere surface arrangement, but in depth.

JOSEPH CAMPBELL, *Myths to Live By* [1]

A T IMPORTANT MOMENTS in life, people, including those who usually show little interest in spirituality, turn to sacred ritual—to celebrate a marriage, to welcome a baby into the world, to say good-bye to a dead loved one. Even those who rarely give God a thought, know that these significant life events require more than just a signature on a piece of paper. Ritual can be helpful too in times of difficulty and stress. When Jaki's husband was rushed to the hospital with an infection in his hand following an injury, she and her two sons were shocked and stunned at his sudden departure. They roamed anxiously around the house, not knowing quite what to do with themselves. Jaki, all at once, sensed what they needed. She gathered her boys around her and, in a quiet family ritual, they lit a candle, spoke about what had just happened and said prayers together. "We sent him our love, and healing," Jaki remembers. "We all felt much better afterward."

The need for sacred ritual runs deeply throughout the history of humankind. We have, as a species, probably always used rituals to invoke spiritual experience. The earliest sacred ritual may have been a community meal shared by prehistoric peoples, during which inedible parts of the kill were burned to provide a pleasing smell to the gods. More than 500,000 years later we eat the bread and drink the wine of the Christian Eucharist, while burning incense.

Ritual throughout the ages has been essential to us, and we may even be born to it. Some biogeneticists believe that ritual is part of our genetic make-up, and that there is a part of our brain that compels us to tap into the energy of the universe through the use of symbols and gestures. Undoubtedly ritual has enormous psychological benefits. It focuses our attention on significant events in our life as they unfold, and helps us give them meaning. Creating a ritual with others produces a tremendous sense of social support, belonging, and unity. It engenders a profound feeling of connection with others, particularly, I have found, when practiced within a group in the form of a circle. Ritual can be therapeutic; for instance, funerals are thought to be a vital part of the grieving process. Psychologists believe that ritual is so powerful because it operates on both a conscious and an unconscious level. A well-performed ritual will always be an emotional experience.

Sacred ritual, however, has been disappearing from modern Western culture. As traditional religion declines, so too do the opportunities to experience collectively our connection to God. People today often think that sacred ritual implies an empty conformity. In church they see a ritual of pomp and circumstance, hear a religious language being spoken that is thousands of years old, and none of it seems to have any current relevance. Children, no doubt, feel even more alienated from traditional worship, which is rarely created with them in mind. Christian churches need radical reform if they are to win back the hearts and minds of people.

Having said that, I do take my children to an Anglican church, where I help coordinate a team that is committed to finding appealing new ways in which families can worship together. When public ritual works it can be a knee-trembling, spine-tingling, transformative experience, and I want my children to be part of it.

But ritual can also be small and private. Mo, a single parent, told me about how she and her son Ryan, age eleven, light two candles on their mantelpiece every evening after dinner, one to pray for themselves and the concerns in their own lives, and the second to pray for people in the wider world. "It was something we started doing after September 11th," Mo remembers. "It felt like the best response we could make to such a terrible event." There is no need for a priest or a shaman to be present when you perform a sacred ritual, just you and any other willing participants amongst family and friends. In Hinduism many sacred rituals take place in the home or at small community shrines. And in Western cultures, this personal home-based ritual practice is in the ascendent. Fresh ideas for rituals have emerged from the New Age movement, some of which are in part a rediscovery of those practiced by peoples in earlier earth-based religions. In an interfaith culture, we are also discovering the beauty of rituals from other religious traditions.

We can make up our own family rituals; they do not need to be preexisting. You can really get creative when designing what you will do together. If that sounds daunting, consider too that rituals do not have to be complicated. You simply need to create a sense of occasion by marking out the space and time as something "other," something set apart from the ordinary. Candles, incense, and flowers may be useful to help you do this. A ritual then requires an intense focus: words, gestures, or actions of some kind that evoke a truth, that touch you deeply. The babble of daily life then fades into the background and for a timeless moment you feel fully present and connected to this truth.

You can use ritual at home to mark a wide range of events. You may want to follow dates of a particular religious calendar, or connect to the rhythms of nature and seasons. Rituals can be used to celebrate special occasions, like birthdays and New Year, and to mark significant milestones such as moving to a new house or starting school. Similarly, death, sickness, and loss can also be acknowledged. The possibilities are many, and with confidence, creativity, and commitment, rituals give families heart, plus provide fun ways to wake ourselves up from the daze of day-to-day activity.

WHY HOME RITUALS NURTURE A FAMILY'S SPIRIT

- ❧ *Rituals create a sense of belonging.* Participants can feel profoundly connected to each other during the shared experience.
- ❧ *Rituals support our spiritual growth.* They present an opportunity to deepen our connection to God and find meaning in life. Psychologists believe they are powerful because they work on both the conscious and the unconscious level.
- ❧ *Rituals calm us down.* Ordinary life stops for a while and we step into a slower place of contemplation.
- ❧ *Rituals encourage emotional release.* Difficult feelings can be transformed and joyful feelings can bubble up. A well-performed ritual will always be an emotional experience.
- ❧ *Rituals connect us to the rhythms of nature.* They can be used to mark the changing seasons and remind ourselves of God's creation.
- ❧ *Rituals affirm important milestones in our lives.* Starting a new school, moving to a new house, becoming a teenager, and important "firsts" can all be marked by rituals. They can also help affirm statements of intention.
- ❧ *Rituals offer comfort at times of distress.* It is known that funerals are therapeutic and an important part of the grieving process. Rituals too may be able to help with other upsetting life experiences, like sickness, separation, and trauma in the world.
- ❧ *Rituals are an opportunity for fun!* Joyful ritual-making is a creative, playful, collective activity, in which we might get to do a little drama, play music, use our imagination, and discover the magic of being alive.

HOW TO CREATE SUCCESSFUL HOME RITUALS WITH CHILDREN

A ritual needs a designer, someone who devises a plan as to what you are going to do together. Initially this will be you or your partner, or possibly another close family member or friend. With time and experience, however, older children may like to try out this role. This person also needs to gather together any materials or objects needed, like candles and pencils. A ritual doesn't always need to be planned. You may find that something spontaneous emerges, especially if you have become accustomed to practicing ritual together as a family.

How to begin

Always begin your ritual by creating a sense of sacred space. It may be enough just to invoke a moment of silence. However, a few "props" are very helpful, especially when trying to engage children.

Candles and incense or scented oils are wonderful aids. Since they were first made 800 years ago, candles have been used for religious ritual and as a focus for meditation. The aroma from incense, scented oils, burning herbs, and scented candles has the power to stimulate us on a deep, unconscious level. Both fire and scented items have been used since ancient times as a way of reaching out to gods. While having a material form here on earth, they are also in part invisible, wafting into the sky and carrying with them our prayers.

Gather your family members into a circle. This can be on the floor on cushions or around a table. We have a long history of sitting in circle formation, since the first peoples gathered around fire for warmth and protection. Placing a candle in the center of the circle possibly connects us back to these ancient memories. There are other ways of marking out a ritual space. You can use flower petals, leaves, ribbons, or pebbles. None of this has to be elaborate: its purpose is simply to acknowledge that you are making a transition into sacred space.

You may want to put on special ceremonial clothes. Religions worldwide have vestments, cloaks, hats, and jewelry used to denote spiritual observance. These have functions far deeper than merely providing social markers. When you use them to their fullest, you become that which you wear; you put on and experience something of the mystery symbolized in the sweep of the cape or the sparkle of an adornment.

My husband and I have started to experiment with wearing colorful shawls when we perform certain rituals. The children seem delighted that we have an opportunity to dress up, and my eldest son has a spectacular wizard hat and cloak that he cheerfully wears for the occasion. The whole thing did seem a little ridiculous at first, but I'm sticking with the process for a while to see whether it will hold any benefits for us.

Hindus, in their group worship, known as Puja, begin with washing the body to symbolize the cleansing of the physical and spiritual being. You may want to experiment with hand-washing before a ritual, using an attractive bowl of petal-strewn water. Hindus also use sound: the ringing of a bell or the chanting of the sacred sound OM (pronounced "Aum").

All these ideas are suggestions, and you may find yourself drawn more strongly to some than others. Give it a try and see what works best with your children.

Keeping it child friendly

Ritual with children has to be very different from ritual created solely for adult participants. Children's attention span is short, so long periods of contemplative silence are generally not recommended. You also have to be mindful that any words, images, or music used have to match their developmental level.

Bearing in mind the following points will ensure a successful ritual with children.

- **Movement.** Don't expect children to sit still for too long, especially if young. You can move around as part of ritual: dance, jump up and down, clap, and use hand gestures.
- **Props.** Draw children into a ritual space by using interesting and relevant objects. This may simply be a candle, or beautiful things from nature; or you can use photographs and appropriate objects. Pulling things sequentially out of a bag often grips them.
- **Active participation.** It's absolutely vital that children have an active part in the ritual. This is not something that you do in their presence, but a process to which they

contribute. Games, artwork, writing activities, singing, and playing percussion instruments all work well.

🌶 **Imagination.** Fire up their imagination with age-appropriate stories and prayers. Puppets and dramatic enactment can also be used to help in the telling.

🌶 **Adult involvement.** You may be leading the celebration, but don't forget to participate fully too. If there are words to be written, pictures to be drawn, or objects to be made, make sure you are creating these as well. During a "circle time" when thoughts are being shared, offering your own ideas often prompts the children.

🌶 **Willingness.** Perform the ritual only if your children are willing. You are unlikely to have a happy experience if they are dragged along screaming and shouting.

How to end

A well-performed ritual needs a sense of completion. What you do depends on the mood that has been created. For a quiet and contemplative final note, try ending on a prayer. For something more upbeat, go for a simple song that the children get to know by heart. The song "He's Got the Whole World in His Hands" is a good one if you are stuck for ideas, and the children can make up verses as you go along. If you are feeling very enthusiastic a big round of applause for yourselves can be appropriate. Gather together for a family puff to extinguish any candles, and watch the smoke rise to the heavens.

Rediscover
Traditional Rituals

When parents and children cultivate traditions that are meaningful to them,
every time they go back to that tradition it renews the emotional energy
and bonding of the past.

STEPHEN R. COVEY, *The 7 Habits of Highly Effective Families*

THE CALENDAR IN western culture is marked by the two crucial Christian celebrations of Christmas and Easter. Even in a
largely secular society, we still take public holidays at these times
and go through the motions of celebration, despite the fact that
for the most part we have forgotten exactly what we are supposed to be feeling joyful about. Reconnect your family to the
deeper meanings of these holiday times and teach your children
about the Christian tradition, which has richly informed the culture in which they are growing up.

CHRISTMAS

Sadly, we have lost much of the original meaning of Christmas in
the frenzy of shopping, eating, and present giving. But the meaning is still there if we look for it, waiting to be found. For Christians
it is a celebration of the birth of Jesus, a savior for the world. Others
may instead celebrate Yuletide (the original name for this festive
time of year), which dates back thousands of years before

Christianity and was a pagan celebration of the rising of the sun following the winter solstice. Yuletide comes from the Germanic word "to turn," referring to the sun, which climbs once again in the sky after its autumn descent. I personally see the Christian and pagan message as ultimately synonymous: birth, God's generosity and love of us, light, warmth, and joy. Take some time to consider what Christmas means to you, and then plan a Christmas with your family that expresses this message. Breathe new life into the usual seasonal rituals by reinventing them if necessary, giving them a twist and new soul flavor. Here are a few ideas.

Celebrate Advent

Children love Advent calendars, which mark the countdown to Christmas, but those of the chocolate, Walt Disney variety do little to convey the rich meanings of the season. Traditionally, Christians mark the four Sundays leading up to Christmas day and the birth of Jesus with the ceremonial lighting of candles on an Advent wreath. Make this ritual your own and use it as a way to slow down during this hectic month and renew your spirits. To make a wreath you need an oasis, five candles, and evergreen foliage. Carve holes in the oasis in which to place the candles (one in the center). My children have great fun doing our wreath, except for the addition of the holly, which is left to me. Find a time on the four Sundays prior to Christmas (after a meal is ideal) to light a candle, one for each week, using the act to focus the family on a particular reflection.

Here is a particularly special advent ritual.[1] It comes from the Unitarian Universalist Family Network, a ministry run by liberal congregations in North America.

Start each lighting with the following words: "Our lighted candle is glowing, making the darkness bright, shining on our family, gathered here tonight."

FIRST SUNDAY

Focus on light and warmth

Introduction: For thousand and thousands of years people have held celebrations at this time of year to mark the return of the sun after the winter cold. We are dependent on the sun for our warmth, light, and food. These celebrations later came to represent the triumph of good over bad and the presence of God.

Reflection: As you look at the candle, think about all the ways in which we depend on the sun and earth. Also think about how the earth depends on us for its care and protection. Invite each family member to make a pledge about how they can take better care of the earth (for example, by recycling paper, turning off light switches).

SECOND SUNDAY
Focus on the miracle of birth

Introduction: Christians think about the birth of Jesus at this time. The birth of every baby is a miracle and, like Jesus, all newborns come with lots of gifts to offer the world.

Reflection: Get out the baby albums and share pictures and memories about the births of your children.

THIRD SUNDAY
Focus on peace

Introduction: One of Jesus's great teachings was that we should love our neighbor as ourselves and do unto others as we would have them do unto us. Similar teachings can be found in all religions.

Reflection: Share examples from your life of ways in which you help make the world a more loving and peaceful place.

FOURTH SUNDAY
Focus on the family

Introduction: The tradition of gift giving at this time of year goes back to ancient peoples, long before there were shops or factories that manufactured things. Share some ideas about what people long ago might have made to give to each other.

Reflection: This is the perfect time to "give inner gifts," as detailed later in this chapter.

Write a different kind of letter to Santa

Instead of the usual list of "I wants" mailed to the North Pole, encourage your child to use the letter for self-reflection too. Ask her to write down all the ways she has been a fantastic human being this year, and possibly remember too a couple of times she did something that she now regrets. Be gentle with this; you don't want your child to feel she is a bad person. When describing Santa to your children focus on his spirit, not his bag of gifts. Use this bearded jolly fellow to teach your children about generosity and unconditional love. Remember that Santa was originally St. Nicholas, a bishop noted for his anonymous gifts to the poor.

Think anew about Christmas cards

You can turn the writing and receiving of cards into a spiritual exercise. Write the cards with your children, and together say a short prayer for each recipient. Similarly, when cards arrive, take a moment at your mealtime to look at the cards together and pray for the sender. You can also share some reminiscences about the good times you have spent with them.

Pledge your services

To reduce the emphasis on material giving, you could start a new ritual where you pledge services to each other. Write these down in Christmas cards and swap. The services will of course depend on the age of your children. The children might offer to wash the car, clean a room, or prepare breakfast one morning. Or they could pledge a performance for you of a piece of music they are practicing, the reading of a poem, or singing of a song. Don't forget that siblings can pledge services to each other too. It could be something as simple as offering to sharpen all their pencils or clean up a messy bookshelf. Adults provide practical services to children every day, so try to offer something more surprising: a performance of some kind, a special outing, a favorite meal.

Give inner gifts

This is a beautiful ritual, best performed when it gets dark in the twinkling light of your Christmas tree. Give every family member an unlit candle and sit in a circle. In the middle place a bowl of sand in which stands one lit candle. Take it in turns to offer each family member heartfelt wishes for the year ahead, and as you do so light your candle and place it in the sand bowl. You might want to wish someone good health so that they can participate in their favorite sport. Or you might want to wish someone the confidence to embark on a new project, or patience when learning a new skill.

Say a special Christmas grace

The big meal is often the heart of the Christmas celebrations. Prepare a special grace for the occasion. The children might like to write one, or draw their prayer as a table centerpiece.

EASTER

Children adore all the fun of Easter with its egg hunts, fluffy chicks, and rabbits. Chocolate and bunnies may on the surface appear to offer few spiritual jewels, but if we look a little closer there are bright sparkles to be seen. As with Christmas, the Christian celebration of Easter also has its roots deeply embedded in pagan earth-based religion. Easter takes its name from Eostar or Ostara, the Germanic goddess of spring, who was worshipped at this time of the year. Eggs are ancient symbols of birth and new beginnings, and rabbits are symbols of fertility for obvious reasons! Easter is a time when the earth is renewing itself, coming back to life after the apparent death of winter. The parallels with the resurrection story are clear.

Take time to consider what Easter means to you. If you are a Christian you may believe in the bodily resurrection of Jesus, or you may take a less literal approach and understand the risen Christ metaphorically, believing that there was no physical resurrection but that the bible story teaches us a great spiritual reality.

It may symbolize to you that there is life after death, that the soul of each person lives on in some mysterious way.

Alternatively, you may want to focus on the spirit of renewal that is giving life to the daffodils and crocuses and drawing animals together to mate. It is the same energy that makes us want to spring-clean the house and get fit after a winter slumbering indoors. For you, the refrain "Christ is risen" may be a call to rise to life and live it to the fullest.

Good Friday

For Christians there can be no Easter without Good Friday, the day that Jesus was crucified on the cross. It is a time when Christians contemplate suffering, pain, and sacrifice. Teaching children about the crucifixion is a difficult matter, since they tend to get fixated on the gore of it all. Undoubtedly it is best to brush over these details with young children, who can become overwhelmed by nightmarish images. Instead focus on what you believe to be the main theological teachings. How does the story of the crucifixion speak to you? Share this with your children. With young children it might be enough to explain that suffering is a part of life and one which, sadly, we cannot avoid, but that God is there with us, helping us carry our burdens, and that we all stand by each other at difficult times. With older children you might want to discuss how when we open ourselves up to love we can also open ourselves up to suffering. The more you love someone, the more it can hurt when that relationship goes wrong or something sad happens to your loved one. Good Friday has many significant messages, which you may revisit differently each year.

GOOD FRIDAY RITUAL

Here is an idea for a simple Good Friday ritual, adapted from something we did at a special children's service at my church.

Prepare a large cardboard cross—corrugated cardboard is ideal. Create a sacred circle with your family by lighting a candle and placing the cross in the center. Cut out a small pile of pieces of paper, black or gray in color, and have glue sticks at the ready.

You might want to make the pieces of paper cross-shaped. If the cross is an empty symbol for you, use another shape, a heart or egg for instance.

Invite your children to write about or draw things in their life that they are finding painful right now. There may be difficulties at school, a health problem, or an unhappy relationship with someone. In turn, stick these on the cross, sharing what has been written. Hold hands and ask God to help all of you cope with the things you find hard.

EASTER SUNDAY RITUAL

This is a ritual to celebrate the renewing power of God's love in our life. Place your cross in the center of your circle again, and this time have ready a pile of colorful paper flower and leaf shapes. Invite your children to write down on the flowers memories about the times in their lives when someone has done something nice for them and shown them love and care. On the leaves, invite them to write down memories about the times they have done something kind for someone else. They then stick the flowers and leaves all over the cross, covering up the painful reflections they had stuck on previously. Finish with a prayer thanking God for all that is good in life.

Create Rituals
for the Seasons

Live in each season as it passes; breathe the air, drink the drink, taste the
fruit, and resign yourself to the influence of each.
HENRY DAVID THOREAU

IT'S EASY TO lose sight of the cycles of nature, especially if we
live in a city. Often we are far more attuned to an annual calendar marked by school holidays and work deadlines than the one
provided to us by the movement of the sun in our sky. People all
around the world have celebrated the changing seasons in some
way. The ancient Celts kept a solar calendar that described the
journey of the sun from the darkness of winter to the full radiance
of summer, and then back again. A solar calendar also determines
the rural year, with its cycle of plowing, sowing, and reaping. We
naturally seem to go through a cycle each year too: we go into a
hibernation-like state in winter, followed by a surge of springtime
energy and the easy living of summer. Here are some family rituals to help you be more aware of these graceful natural changes.

WINTER SOLSTICE

This occurs on December 21, the shortest day of the year. It cele-
brates the change from the shortest day to the beginning of the

lengthening ones. Even in the dark of winter there is the promise of sunshine to come. People traditionally create light at this time. Pagans and Christians decorate evergreen trees with twinkling lights and glittering ornaments, and Jewish people light candles for eight nights. Some pagans may stay up all night to keep the Mother Goddess company as she labors to give birth to the sun. If your family is highly enthusiastic you could wake up in time to watch the dawn. Seek a high vantage point for maximum effect. For a less demanding celebration, you could paint or draw images of the sun and hang them up for decoration. Have a conversation with your children about the sun and its tremendous importance. Go outside and look at it, being careful not to hurt your eyes. Tell your children about where it rises and sets in relation to their home. It's surprising how many children have absolutely no knowledge of this. If you are all feeling especially cheerful, sing "Happy Birthday" to the sun.

For a different approach you may wish instead to concentrate on the long dark night by performing a "dream incubation" ritual. This idea comes from Anne Hill, one of the authors of *Circle Round*,[1] a book about raising children in the goddess traditions. Set the scene: a quiet relaxed evening in a cozy room, gentle music, and warm milk. Pajamas, blankets, and sleeping bags should be brought to the gathering and everyone should settle in around a big bowl of water and a candle. Family members should come with either a question to "put" into the water, or an object symbolizing something in their lives they would like dream-help for. In this ritual you are inviting the family to journey deep into their unconscious and bring forth a dream that will help them in the year ahead.

Everyone takes a turn to speak a question into the water. This could be written on a piece of paper and dropped in, or spoken aloud while dipping in a hand: "We ask for a dream to show us where to go in the coming year," for example.

Anne Hill suggests that you all sleep together in your ritual space, but if this seems too uncomfortable and the kids are too frisky to sleep, you could all go to your own beds, making sure you have paper and pens ready to jot down dreams upon waking. To complete the process, gather again in the morning to share your dreams and find what wisdom you can in them. In the words of the poet Kahlil Gibran, "Trust your dreams, for in them is hidden the gate to eternity."

SPRING EQUINOX

Day and night are of equal length at the spring equinox, on March 21. After this, every day becomes longer until midsummer. The equinox can occur round about Easter (which takes its name from the Germanic goddess Eostar—see page 66). As well as springtime themes of hope and new life, the theme of "balance" is also examined at this time, particularly the balance between life and death. During the winter solstice the sun is thought to be reborn; during the spring equinox the earth is thought to be reborn. Eggs are an old symbol of birth and renewal, so an Easter egg hunt is as good a way as any of celebrating the spring equinox. For a craft activity you can paint eggs and use them as decorations. To hollow out an egg, gently pierce a hole in both ends and blow out the contents.

Seed planting with children is a meaningful springtime activity: you could plant some in broken eggshells in egg boxes to combine two images of new life. Ask your children to write their names on small pieces of paper and bury them alongside the seeds. As the seeds grow into plants, encourage your children to see that they too are blossoming.

SUMMER SOLSTICE

This occurs in midsummer, on the longest day of the year, June 21. Summer is in full bloom, the crops are growing and there are still plenty of days of sunshine to look forward to (and the summer holidays too). Life is good, nature is generous. It's time to party and count our blessings! The summer solstice celebration is customarily a chance to rest and play a little before the harvest needs to be gathered in. Traditionally bonfires are lit and people may stay up all night with the fire.

To celebrate nature's abundance make an altar of flowers with the children: this may be as simple as an arrangement in a vase (sunflowers are very appropriate) or you may want to go to town with the addition of orange candles and summer fruits. Gather around your altar to count your blessings. Ask everyone to write down, or draw, the things in their lives for which they feel grateful. Place them on the altar. Favorite toys and photos of treasured people and pets can also find their way there too. This lovely ritual can be performed outside, weather permitting. To really make a night of it, camp and build a bonfire.

AUTUMN EQUINOX

The days and nights are again of equal length on September 21, the autumn equinox. This is harvest time, and the beginning of the earth going back to darkness and winter again. Traditionally it is a time to give our thanks to the earth for yet another year of grain, fruit, and vegetables.

Have fun making an autumn altar, with sweet corn, pumpkins, wheat, or barley (if you can get it). Autumn leaves, if they have started to turn, and candles in brown hues all carry the theme well. Vote on what is the family's favorite meal and serve it, with a thanksgiving prayer to precede.

For an alternative celebration, Diane Baker, another author of *Circle Round*, says she takes her family to explore a place in nature they have never been to before. "We are overt about making this trip for a sacred purpose," she says. They gather things from nature, like pine cones, pretty seed heads, and leaves, and string them together on twigs to make a mobile. This is hung from the branch of a tree, with a thank you to the earth for all its beautiful and varied gifts.

Create Rituals
for Other Festivities

There's a party goin' on right here, A celebration to last throughout the
years. So bring your good times, and your laughter too, We gonna celebrate
and have a good time. It's time to come together, it's up to you, what's your
pleasure. Everyone around the world come on!

> KOOL AND THE GANG, *from the song "Celebrate"*

MANY OF THE usual secular festivities we enjoy each year
can be used as opportunities to share a spiritual experience
with your children. These rituals are simple and require little
preparation or planning. Just bring a candle or two—and your
willingness to make the moment magic.

NEW YEAR'S EVE

Since having children, my husband and I have temporarily given
up on the usual New Year's Eve partying. A lack of babysitters
and general exhaustion are the main reasons why we find ourselves at home at midnight each December 31. However, an interesting alternative celebration has emerged. As well as having a
nice meal and a bottle of champagne, we use the evening to think
about the highs and lows of the year just lived, and to consider
what we would like our life to be like in the year to come. Here is
a way you could celebrate this style of ritual together, at midnight, or earlier if the children are too young for such a late night.

A New Year's Eve Sharing

Create a sacred space by gathering in a circle, with a candle and metal bowl in the middle. Have your family calendar there for the year just gone, and also one for the year to come. Go through each month, sharing happy and sad memories, and when everyone has spoken burn the relevant calendar page. When this is finished, make your resolutions for the new year and write them on the new calendar as a reminder. At midnight share hugs and blessings, and a glass of bubbly for those old enough.

MOTHER'S DAY AND FATHER'S DAY

Cynically, we may believe that Mother's Day and Father's Day were created by the greetings card industry, but honoring parents has its roots in many religious traditions. It is the instruction of the Fifth Commandment. "Show kindness to your parents," spoke Muhammad. And in Jewish mystical writing: "Honor your father and mother, even as you honor God, for all three were partners in your creation."

Mother's Day possibly began in ancient Greece, when Rhea, the mother of the gods, was celebrated. Today, all around the world, on different days, there is a date in the calendar set aside to give thanks to mothers. In seventeenth-century Britain it was a holiday during which servants and apprentices living away from home could return for a family visit.

Today we typically give thanks to mothers with cards, flowers, and small gifts. Dads get cards and presents too, on Father's Day, but flowers are less common, mistakenly thought to be unmanly. Many schools invite children to make a Mother's Day card, and each one I have delighted in and kept for posterity in my memory chest.

Sadly, dads seem to lose out here, since schools are very sensitive to the fact that some children don't have contact with their fathers.

Both occasions are a great opportunity for you to encourage your children to show their appreciation for their parents, and to create a mindful moment during which they can reflect upon the love they receive from you.

The Mommy/Daddy "thank you" pot

A few days before Mother's or Father's Day, put out a pot, jar, or piggy bank and invite your children to write "thank you" notes to drop inside (then pray hard that they put something in!). Children can write these whenever an idea pops into their head. "Thank you for making my sandwiches," "thank you for reading me a story," "thank you for mending my toy." The possibilities are many, but may need the encouragement of an adult to help them along. You could decorate the pot with a photo of the parent to be appreciated. The notes may need to be written by an adult if the child is young. I realize that single parents are at a disadvantage here, but a friend or grandparent might be willing to help.

On the day itself, create a ritual space by sitting in a circle around a candle. Mom or dad then reads aloud the "thank you" notes, one at a time. Take time to read each one, really letting its love and gratitude enter into you. You may wish to finish with a prayer, song, or round of applause.

HALLOWEEN

Children really enjoy Halloween with all its scary costumes and pumpkin lanterns. It seems to be celebrated in an increasingly commercial way, with all kinds of spooky merchandise on sale in the shops at this time of year. Halloween is a melting pot of several ancient sacred festivals. First it comes from the Celts, who celebrated Samhaim, the final feast of the year before the world was thought to die. They wore ugly costumes and built fires in the belief that they could scare away evil spirits. Then the Romans conquered and Samhaim merged with the Roman harvest celebration of Pomona, in which the goddess of orchards was honored. Apple bobbing is a tradition that comes from this time. Finally, in 835 the Roman Catholic Church took over the festival, transforming it into All Hallows Eve, the night before All Saints' Day, in which the lives of Christian saints are celebrated. The following day is All Souls' Day, a time to remember those who have died, especially family members.

Some Christian fundamentalists get worked up about

Halloween, claiming that it encourages children to dabble in black magic and what they perceive as dangerous paganism. I personally think it's extremely healthy to have at least one time in the year when we think about death and face our fears in a playful and joyful way. Talk to your children about the history of Halloween, and as well as your usual costume capers you might want to try the following ideas.

Remember your ancestors

Use Halloween as a chance to talk with your children about members of the family who have died. Get out photos if you have them. Older children might like to draw up a family tree with the help of living grandparents. Sam Collins, who facilitates family experience weeks at the holistic education center Monkton Wyld Court in Dorset, UK, told me that she had successfully created a "table of honor for ancestors," in which families were encouraged to place mementos of dead loved ones. "Children brought pictures of fish and rabbits, and in some cases little brothers and sisters. It was very moving, and they really seemed to enjoy it," she said.

Go on an owl prowl or a bat hunt

If you know of a spot where these night creatures can be found, this is the perfect night to try and see them. Carry candles in jam jars for maximum atmospherics. Many local nature groups offer organized night walks at this time of year.

BIRTHDAYS

Birthdays are a very special day in a child's annual calendar. Mine seem to look forward to them for months ahead, and chatter optimistically about how old they will be, what presents they would like, and who they will invite to their party. A big priority is always given to the birthday cake and its presentation when everyone sings "Happy Birthday." I can't think of any other time in life when a room full of people sing you a blessing of best wishes and love.

The birthday candle ritual

This simple ritual was suggested to me by Jaki Harris, who runs spiritual parenting workshops in the UK. We tried it for the first time this year for my daughter's third birthday, and it was a truly lovely moment that everyone enjoyed and that brought a huge lump to my throat.

While the family are gathered at the table (a good moment may be after presenting the birthday cake), take a candle (big enough to hold in your hand without drips) and pass it from person to person. As you hold the candle, tell the birthday child something you like or love about him or her. End with "Happy Birthday," and a round of applause.

SPIRITUAL LIFE TOGETHER

Say Grace
at Mealtimes

I don't want you just to sit down at the table.
I don't want you just to eat, and be content.
I want you to walk out into the fields
where the water is shining, and the rice has risen.
I want you to stand there, far from the white tablecloth.
I want you to fill your hands with the mud, like a blessing.

MARY OLIVER, *from her poem "Rice"*[1]

THERE'S NOTHING LIKE a table of tasty food to bring a family together. It's a time-honored tradition to offer God prayers at this time to express our gratitude for what we are about to eat, and many believe giving thanks to God for food was probably humanity's first act of worship. Every religion and spiritual tradition has rituals and prayers connected to food. Such prayers have taken on a very profound significance in the Christian Holy Communion and Jewish Seder celebrations. In traditional Hindu belief, food cannot be eaten until it is first offered to God. Buddhism has a slightly different approach, commanding a thankfulness for food by a vow to live a life that is worthy to receive it. The Native Americans ask a plant or animal for forgiveness in taking its life, explaining why the sacrifice is necessary.

Alas, in recent years the habit of giving thanks for food has gone out of fashion. Saying grace has been abandoned by most in the West as a quaint and pious ritual that has no place in the modern world. Food now is fast, often eaten on the move, something that fuels our bodies but not our souls. Some families rarely gather together to eat food and instead are splintered into solitary dining by the demands of long working hours, the lure of the television, and a hectic after-school activity schedule. According to one survey, a quarter of families only get to sit down and eat together once a month, and only 15 percent manage it every day.

Mealtimes are a very important and enjoyable way to gather as a family and share news about the day: in many ways they represent the heart of family life. Taking a moment to say grace adds a deeper level of meaning to the occasion because it makes us aware that the food in front of us is a gift. There is bounty in the world, and here on the table lies the proof. Briefly we might contemplate the sun and rain that gave the food life, the human hands that brought it to harvest and stacked it on the supermarket shelf, and finally the person who cooked it. In its fullest sense saying grace is a beautiful act of awareness about our connection to the forces of nature and each other. There's something sacramental about sharing food together, and it feels utterly right to have a prayer at that time. I honestly believe that food tastes better when we have had a moment of contemplation, as we are allowing it to enter our being more fully.

We started saying grace with our children when they were very young, and it was soon apparent that this was a devotion that they enjoyed, and even asked for. On good days, that is. Like much of life with young children, it is rarely a predictable or orderly affair. Grace is often said while hungry children are either already munching or wailing loudly that they don't like the menu for that night. A cup of juice might be spilled midprayer, or someone might announce that they need to go to the toilet *now*. But we do our best, and that's OK. On the good days we all hold hands, and different family members will spontaneously give thanks for the food, and often anything else that comes to mind. Once my eldest son asked us to thank God for "poo poo and wee wee." So we did.

We might also think about those who are less fortunate and do not have food to eat. Children can become very accomplished at this family ritual from a young age. The other day my daughter Iona, age three, cheerfully led a large table of diners in the most beautiful grace, which she spontaneously composed.

We make a habit of saying grace when we all eat together at

weekends but, as in many families, dining is more fragmented during the week. However, I do often offer a short prayer when the children are sitting down to eat dinner on their own. There is definitely a discipline to it. Sometimes it can feel like one more chore to be done before you get to your grub, but once said, I never regret having taken the moment. Even a few words and a couple of seconds of reflection have the power to transcend the busyness of daily life.

I can feel self-conscious about saying grace when there are other people dining with us who are not accustomed to prayer. Saying grace in a pizza restaurant is even more daunting. In someone else's house even worse. There are no easy answers that I know of, other than being selective about when you say grace, saying it silently, or having the courage of your convictions and carrying on regardless. Grace is a spiritual opportunity for the family that is simply too good to be missed. Discover this traditional ritual, rework it if you need to, and make it your own.

HOW TO SAY GRACE

- ❥ Create a conducive space by making sure everyone is sitting at the table, and the television is off.
- ❥ Hold hands when you say grace. It creates a tremendous sense of unity.
- ❥ Keep grace short—you don't want the kids to get too hungry or the food to get cold.
- ❥ When you first start, an adult will need to lead the prayer, but in time children can take on that role too.
- ❥ Vary the wording so that grace doesn't become boring. Try a spontaneous grace that everyone can add to, run through the range of possible variations with a written grace.
- ❥ Try writing your own grace, or ask older children to write one.
- ❥ If you are feeling very bold, try a sung grace. Young children especially love the opportunity to sing.
- ❥ A silent grace might feel more appropriate sometimes (but only with older children who have learned how to practice the ritual).

- Invite your children to paint and draw pictures of food and bring them to the table as a thanksgiving prayer.
- A "silly" grace is good to use when everyone is in a light-hearted mood (or you have a guest who feels uncomfortable with prayer).
- For special meals light a candle as part of the ritual of saying grace.
- Remember, it may seem awkward at first, but the more experience you have of saying grace, the easier and more natural it becomes for everyone to take part in this special family moment.

THE GRACE LUCKY DIP

Introduce an element of play into your table prayers by making a "grace lucky dip." Get everyone to write down their favorite table prayers on separate pieces of card and put them into a bag. A blank card can represent a silent grace. Each mealtime take it in turns to close your eyes and pick out the grace to be read. I have found that this playful device really focuses the children and keeps the ritual alive.

A "TASTER" ANTHOLOGY OF GRACE

Thank you for the world so sweet;
Thank you for the food we eat;
Thank you for the birds that sing;
Thank you, God, for everything.
    E. Rutter Leatham[2]

Let us take a moment
To thank God for our food,
for friends around the table
And everything's that good.
    Lois Rock[3]

For what we are about to receive, may God make us truly thankful.
    Traditional

We are thankful for this meal,
The work of many people
And the sharing of other forms of life.
      Zen prayer

Rub a dub dub, thank God for this grub.
    Anonymous

Give thanks to the Mother Earth.
Give thanks to the Father Sun.
Give thanks to the plants in the garden
Where the mother and father are one.
    Grace used in Rudolf Steiner schools

Hold
Family Meetings

Who speaks, sows; who listens, reaps.
TRADITIONAL FRENCH SAYING

I F YOU WANT good communication with your children, one of the best ways of promoting this is to organize a regular family meeting. Organizations and businesses could not work effectively if meetings weren't called to discuss important issues, and the same is also true of the family. Such meetings have long been advocated by parenting experts as an excellent way of sharing meaningful conversation, problem solving, planning life together, and creating a sense of unity. You can use the time to clear the air after a squabble, plan the summer vacation, discuss division of chores, and share news. If you are a spiritual parent you can in addition use family meetings as an opportunity to create a sacred space and go together into a deeper place beyond the everyday.

Ideally, family meetings should be set at a regular time each week or month, depending on your preferred frequency and time constraints. Friday evening after dinner or Sunday afternoon are times that might be appropriate. Meetings work best with school-age children, but younger ones might be able to participate, especially if the meeting is kept short and you generate as much fun as possible. If you are a small family there is no reason why you can't also hold a meeting: if there are two of you, there are enough. Every family can develop its own structure, but here are some suggestions.

PREPARE A SPECIAL SPACE TO MEET

Slumping on the sofa with the TV on in the background is not going to promote anything much more significant than a few halfhearted grunts at each other. Instead, remove all distractions, including the telephone. Meeting around a dining room or kitchen table works very well. Alternatively, you could set up a circle of cushions on the floor, or even in the garden during the summer. Clear away surrounding clutter and choose a center-piece as a focus for your family circle. The candle has a long association with spiritual practices and creates a special, intimate atmosphere. Flowers and other beautiful objects from nature, like seashells and crystals, are always uplifting. You might want to find an object that you use each time, or run through the range of possible variations. Alternatively, let each family member in turn find, or make, your meeting centerpiece.

STRUCTURING THE MEETING

Start your meeting with a prayer or a few moments of silence. Hold hands, if that feels right. You might want to give God thanks for this special time that you are about to share together, and ask for God's help in making decisions wisely and speaking with respect and love to each other. You could memorize a common prayer that you use each time. Take it in turns to put onto the "agenda" any issues that you would like to discuss. If things get very lively someone might need to act as a chair (it doesn't always have to be a parent). Or if everyone is talking over the top of each other, you could circulate a talking stick, much as Native Americans traditionally do. This is passed around the group, either in turn or as requested, and only the person holding it can speak. Children love the power of holding it!

Make lists and take notes if it is helpful: have a special family journal that you bring out for such occasions. If the family has had little opportunity to share news, this is a fantastic place to do so. Try to keep the meeting upbeat and optimistic rather than letting it sink into a quagmire of complaints. You could take it in turns to share something you have appreciated about each family member since you last met. "I really appreciated you cleaning your room," or "It was really good of you to read a bedtime story to your little sister." Reinforcing positive behavior works wonderfully with children. Encourage each other and heap praises.

WHEN THERE'S PAIN AND CONFLICT

Every family has its disagreements and this is an excellent arena in which to discuss them openly. To ensure that any anger doesn't become destructive you might want to set some ground rules, like no nasty name calling or harsh words. The talking stick is a useful tool in these situations because it ensures that people don't interrupt each other and that everyone gets a fair turn at saying their piece. You could take a moment to pray and ask God to help you find the best way forward, or ask God to help heal the differences between you.

Something useful, which my husband introduced me to, was the use of a bell as a "slowing down" tool. We use Tibetan bells, which have a beautiful resonance. Appoint one member of the group to be the guardian of the bell. If things are getting too heated or people are talking on top of each other, the guardian can ring the bell to signal a short moment of silence. The bell is then rung to resume dialogue. The bell can be rung in the same way if someone has shared something really personal and important that deserves a moment of reflection.

MAKE IT FUN

If your meeting has as much fizz and fun as possible, the children will keep coming back for more. Plan something enjoyable that you will all do together before you next sit down to meet. It might be a day out, a video and popcorn evening, or a favorite meal. Children sometimes enjoy the simplest things: mine often ask to have a picnic in the car because they love pulling down the little tables set in the backs of the seats. Or, after your discussion time, you could play a family game together. This might be a board game, cards, or charades. Perhaps there's a story that could be read aloud. Throw a surprise occasionally. At his family meetings, David Robinson, a pastor who has written about using Benedictine wisdom in the home, says he has got everyone to make their own banana split, produced a gift-wrapped book to read, shared stories about embarrassing experiences, and created a "clown of the week" award.[1] You could finish the family meeting with a song: this is especially enjoyed by younger children.

TROUBLESHOOTING

A possible pitfall, especially with older children, is that someone doesn't want to have a meeting because it's "silly" or "boring," or "a waste of time." Insisting that family members participate is likely to make them resent the meeting and rebel yet more. Instead, let them know that important family decisions will be made at the meeting, and that if they don't attend they won't be able to have their say on the matter. Warmly let them know that their presence will be missed, and tell them how much you enjoy them being there. You might need to reassess whether you have had enough fun recently at your meetings, and also whether the balance has swung too far toward moaning and complaining. Of course, the person not wanting to attend could be one of the parents, and in this case the same recommendations apply. However, it only needs one parent present to hold a family meeting, which is good news for the single parent.

THE FAMILY ANNUAL GENERAL MEETING

Once a year hold a meeting that is extra special—your AGM. This is a time when you can look back over the year and assess your struggles and triumphs. Read back through the family journal together and share congratulations all round. Did someone learn how to ride a bike this year, or swim without floaties, or take part in a school performance? With growing children the lists of new achievements are many and varied. Think of the year ahead and plan some family goals and happy events to look forward to. You could invite extended family members to your AGM: grandparents, aunts and uncles, godparents, and close friends. Sharing food together makes a great finale.

Make Story Time Magic

The only books that influence us are those for which we are ready, and which have gone a little farther down our particular path than we have yet got ourselves.

E.M. FORSTER, *Two Cheers for Democracy*

ONCE UPON A time a spiritually minded parent had half an hour of quality time to spend with his two elementary-school-aged children. The good father thought long and hard about how he could best nourish his children's souls in thirty minutes. There seemed to him to be three meaningful options. He could: a) read his children fairy stories, b) get out atlases and picture books and teach them something factual about the world, or c) give them some explicit moral and religious instruction, and say prayers. Which should he choose? This is the dilemma that the radical theologian Don Cupitt used to open a conference held in the UK in 2003 by the liberal Christian network, The Sea of Faith. Cupitt, an eminent, well-published thinker, believes that this father would make the wisest choice by going for the first option, fairy stories. "In order to understand life and in order to imagine, choose, and live out a meaningful life of our own, we need to carry with us a large stock of stories," explained Cupitt. He went on to argue that the fantastical settings of fairy stories and tales like Beatrix Potter's achieve a faraway, long ago, and different

PARENTING WITH SPIRIT

world backdrop that, unlike everyday life, has the ability to slip past our natural resistance to accepting advice. In other words, an earnest talk with your child about how telling lies will get her into trouble is less likely to be taken to heart than a captivating rendition of the Aesop's fable "The Boy Who Cried Wolf."

Children and adults alike hunger for a good story. It is an appetite that is probably nearly as old as our ability to speak: the most ancient written records and primitive tribal cultures both show evidence of our story-making skills. For countless generations, children have been tucked into bed with a lovingly told story. This intimate family moment can be an incentive for working parents to race home, and is often the only way in which tired children will relinquish their wide-eyed hold on the world.

Leaving your child to listen to a story on an audiotape may be enjoyable for a child and easy for a parent, but it can in no way capture this magic, because children's bedtime stories are as much about the intimacy between the teller and the listener as about the tale itself. If you have had a stressful day, this is an opportunity for healing, because on your lap or tucked beneath your arms, your children feel safe and loved. Together you share a story that is like warm milk, feeding your child's imagination and understanding of the world.

CHOOSING BOOKS

You might be asking if that is really what is going on when you read that Thomas the Tank Engine book for the twentieth time. But a cozy cuddle with Thomas the Tank Engine may be just what your child needs right now. Children require stories that speak to many different aspects of their being: funny stories, down-to-earth stories, adventure stories, whimsical stories, fantastical stories, stories about life events that a child might be experiencing. But a spiritual parent is also looking out for that special story containing a power that will impact on the higher parts of a child's imagination and reveal sacred truths. These are more difficult to find, but they are out there, written for all ages. Even simple picture books for the youngest readers can have the power to cast such a spell.

How can a parent find such books? Choosing books for children is a bewildering experience because of the sheer volume available: 4,000 to 5,000 new children's books are published in the United States each year.

You probably already know some of the best ones, because they may have been the books that impacted on you when you were a child, and have survived the test of time to become classics. Those that still ignite a flame in my memory include *The Chronicles of Narnia* by C. S. Lewis, *The Secret Garden* by Frances Hodgson Burnett, *Tom's Midnight Garden* by Philippa Pearce, *Pollyanna* by Eleanor H. Porter, and *The Wizard of Oz* by L. Frank Baum.[1] Modern children's fiction is harder to navigate, but children's book awards (like the Carnegie Medal, The Whitbread Children's Book of the Year, the Smarties Book Prize and The Guardian Award for Children's fiction) may give some assurance of quality. *Skellig* by David Almond and *Waiting for Mermaids* by Sue Welford have both been reliably recommended to me.[2]

Picture books can be quickly skimmed before loan or purchase to evaluate contents. I know I have found something of a higher order when I feel a lump in my throat and my eyes well up; you no doubt will have your own signals. Those I have found especially moving include *The Big Big Sea* by Martin Waddell, *Guess How Much I Love You* by Sam McBratney and Anita Jeram, *The Rainbow Fish* by Marcus Pfister, and *The Velveteen Rabbit* by Margery Williams. Another parent I know never fails to cry when he reads *The Selfish Giant* by Oscar Wilde.[3]

A spiritual parent will be looking out for books with a positive message, that affirm the essential goodness and wonder of life. Thematically, stories proclaim the power of love and friendships, and champion human virtues like courage, compassion, generosity, honesty, and helpfulness. Be cautious about those that overly dwell on frightening and macabre detail, and take care not to overtax your child's emotions with material that may give them nightmares.

Hilary Foster chooses and reviews books for Words of Discovery,[4] a British mail order company specializing in children's holistic, spiritual, and personal development books (which I highly recommend). She is also the literacy advisor for Leicester

City Local Education Authority. I asked her for advice on what to look for when choosing children's books, and here she offers a number of questions you might want to ask yourself.

- *Is the book pleasing to the eye?* Choose those that are well made and illustrated.
- *Is it well written?* Take a few moments, reading a couple of pages, to look at the language and judge whether it is well crafted.
- *What issues does it address?* A read of the synopsis on the back cover will give you a good idea. Look out for books with purpose that may help children understand concepts that are bigger than day-to-day issues.
- *Does it have a positive message?* Be clear about your own values and know what messages you want your children to read. Hilary advises looking at how the book ends to ascertain how issues are resolved.
- *Will it stimulate my child's imagination?* "You can't preach to kids," says Hilary. "You have to give them imaginative situations in which they can pick up the positive message in their own language and level of understanding."
- *Is my child showing interest in this book?* Allow your children to have choice in what they read. There will be little joy in reading something that does not excite them. With young children you can control the range of books offered to them, but your influence wanes as they get older. "They will want to try a whole range of books," says Hilary. "The issues may not be positive or written about in positive way, and the best you can do is be available to talk with them about it."

SPIRITUAL STORIES FROM AROUND THE WORLD

I have started up a new ritual in our household on Friday evenings. It is called hot chocolate night. Instead of story time taking place in separate bedrooms with individual children, we all gather together, around the fire in winter, for hot chocolate and a story. I try to find a sacred story for the occasion, and at the moment we are enjoying together a collection of Bible stories written especially to be read aloud to children. If you think Bible stories are dull, look again. Many contain tremendous drama and action to enthrall children, if they are told in engaging and appropriate language. There are many other sacred stories that I look forward to sharing, including those from other faith traditions: Hindu and Buddhist, Muslim, Taoist, Sufi, Native American, and Aboriginal.[5] Anthologies of these stories for children are hard to find at the moment in Britain, and you may have to order from the United States.[6] There can be much wisdom in these ancient tales, which have been passed down from generation to generation.

So how should we encourage our children to understand sacred stories? For me, a statement like this makes a useful preface: "I do not know whether the events in this story happened or not, but I believe there are truths in it." This is a declaration similar to one suggested by Marcus Borg, a professor of religion and culture at Oregon State University and author of many theological books. He describes scripture and sacred story as "not something to be believed in, but a means for mediating the sacred. That is, scripture is not to be treated as an object of belief but is to be lived within. It becomes a lens through which we 'see' God, life, and ourselves and a means by which our imaginations are shaped by the sacred."[7]

After you have read the story to your children, you might want to ask them a few questions about it that help reveal the truths contained within. For instance, if it was the story of the Good Samaritan, you might ask your children what they would do if they found someone hurt on the roadside, and why.

FAIRY TALES

There has been a long debate in education about the pros and cons of telling fairy stories to children. The Waldorf Education system has especially valued the place of folklore in childhood. "Much deeper than one might imagine lie the sources whence flow genuine, true folk tales that speak their magic throughout all centuries of human evolution," said Rudolf Steiner. Proponents of fairy stories believe that they are populated by rich archetypal characters and speak wisely about the good human world that lies beyond the wickedness of giants, dragons, and witches. They are also a powerful way to unleash a child's imagination. Great old tales like "Cinderella," "Beauty and the Beast," "Snow White," and "The Ugly Duckling" have long been treasured by children, who are spellbound by the enchanted world they describe. It is a magnetic place that adults and children can return to again and again, to explore safely feelings such as jealousy, anger, laziness, and greed. They can then journey onward to a positive resolution, and in so doing commune with those human virtues that are needed to get to the "happily ever after" ending.

Critics of children's fairy stories point out that they are often violent and horrific. Many a character has been gobbled up by a wolf, and some believe that in the original "Sleeping Beauty" the heroine was awoken not by a chaste kiss but, shockingly, by the onset of childbirth—twin babies that had been conceived while she slumbered. It has to be remembered that these tales, which were told (rather than read) during long evenings by the crackling fireside, were originally intended for adults. It was only during the Victorian era that they were appropriated for children, and consequently still need to be approached with some caution. I personally love the way in which these tales connect us back to storytellers of the past, and I value sharing their moral code with my children. Those stories with wings, which inhabit the fairy realm, allow us to take flight from the everyday and open ourselves up to the possibility of transcendent experiences. They speak to our yearning for the divine. We can also often confidently tell familiar fairy tales without needing to read a book, which leads us on to the next installment of our tale.

STORYTELLING WITHOUT BOOKS

It is only in relatively recent years that families have had access to such a wealth of books. In times before the printed page was so readily available, parents instead used to make up stories for their offspring. The oral tradition of storytelling has largely disappeared, and parents have probably lost their confidence in being able to create their own wondrous tales rich in words, images, and plot. However, there is something of a storytelling revival going on, with interested groups and individuals attempting to reclaim this lost art. Nancy Mellon is a Waldorf teacher, psychotherapist, and teacher of children's storytelling, and if you are interested in finding out more about this subject, her book *Storytelling with Children* is seminal reading.[8] "Storytelling is different from reading stories," she explains. "Storytelling comes more directly from the self. It's not only good for children, but necessary for at least one person in their life who can really nurture them with whole narratives and tell them about their family life, and tell them stories that are just for them." Nancy Mellon believes that when we bring forth our own stories for children we are sharing more of ourselves, which she sees as infinitely more valuable than fiction stacked in their rooms. "It brings emotional closeness and a physical comfort. It's so important to have an adult who is really there for them, not looking into a book, but looking at them and sharing soul speech," she says. The other benefit of this type of storytelling is that we are demonstrating to our children the creative process: if we can create our own stories, then so can they.

Your ability to conjure up wonderful stories for your children might take you by surprise, as it did Vasco, who after a stressful day working as a high school teacher still finds the energy to go on great imaginative voyages when he puts his three young children to bed. "I got the idea that I might be able to make up my own stories from a parenting class we went to. I started out with my eldest daughter Phoebe, and she absolutely loved it," he says. Now he has to make up stories every night for her and his middle child Jevan. Vasco invents fantastical stories about his own childhood, like the day he came home from school to find a giraffe in his back garden. He has also expanded his repertoire to include fantasy stories about the children's grandfather, who grew up in India. "It means I can get jungles and tigers in there," he says. Recently he had a three-night epic in which he went on a dragon hunt and encountered stone dragons, cloud dragons, and mountain dragons. "I've got a tear-shaped crystal around my neck, and the punch line of the story was that it was a dragon's tear."

Nancy Mellon suggests that there are several different types of storytelling you might try:

What happened today

Go over the details of your child's day as if it were a story, with a beginning, middle, and end. It helps children assimilate their day, and they love hearing their experiences being put warmly into words. You might want to add some imaginary flourishes, or give the protagonist a different name and identity to their own. Says Nancy: "Hearing us speak about their accomplishments, feelings, and discoveries, they weave their experiences into a nest of understanding and dreams."

STORYTELLING TIPS

➤ Light a large candle to mark your storytelling, and ceremoniously extinguish it to mark the end of your time together.

➤ Have a stock of shawls and blankets that you can wrap around yourselves at story time.

➤ You could mark the beginning and end of story time with a musical instrument, like jingling bells or a xylophone. Traditionally, storytellers used to play a lyre.

➤ Bedtime is a natural story moment, but consider other times of the day too. You could for instance have a weekly Sunday morning story, or a Friday evening pajama party with stories. Special days could also be marked by stories, like the summer solstice, Mother's Day, Christmas Eve, or Easter Sunday.

➤ Puppets and soft toys are useful props to help you tell a story. Also consider using objects like leaves, flowers, family photos, and other artifacts that may be appropriate to the story. Pulling them out of a bag or basket sequentially as the tale is told holds a child's attention.

➤ Practice the art of storytelling. Believe that there is a storyteller in you, have the confidence to give it life, and watch your skills and confidence grow as you share this joyful time with your children.

Personal memories

There are lots of little anecdotal tales that we could tell our children about our own childhood and (if you know about them) the childhood of grandparents and great grandparents. Preserve your family lore by reciting these personal stories. You might want to tell them about a favorite game, pet, hiding place, holiday, adventure, or toy. Try to hold your characters in respect and kindness, and look for the positive silver threads woven into any dark cloth of adversity. You might want to narrate the story from the perspective of an observer, like a big old tree that stood in the garden, or a little mouse that lived in the baseboard of your house.

Spontaneous storytelling

You need to be willing to launch yourself out onto the waves of your imagination for this type of storytelling, in which you create your own make-believe. Like Vasco, you may be delighted to find that these waters are filled with sunken treasure.

Spontaneous storytelling can evolve into a creative collaboration between you and your children in which you respond intuitively to their needs at the time, putting your imagination at their service. They might want to contribute to the story as it goes along, an enjoyable process that binds you closely together. If you are worried that you can't make up a story as good as those found in books, Nancy Mellon warns against being held back by your fears. "Children sense sincere creative effort," she says. "They love this as a reflection of their own growing and striving."

Storytelling without a book

One of the joys of oral storytelling is that you do not have a book between you and your children. You can face your children as you tell the story, look into their faces and whisk them along with hand gestures and different dramatic voices. You embody the story more fully than when you read it. To learn a story read it aloud to yourself several times. You might want to tape yourself telling the story and play it back to hear and improve your story-telling style.

It may help you to remember the story if you visualize it in a series of pictures. Imagine each scene in detail as if it were being playacted, noticing the colors and costumes, words and gestures. Let it plant its seeds of wisdom, truth, beauty, joy, or sadness in your soul, and trust that all this goodness will flower into a com-pelling story bouquet for you to give to your little ones.

15

Use Visualization
with Your Children

Imagination is a very high sort of seeing.

RALPH WALDO EMERSON

WHEN HILARY PUTS her five-year-old daughter Maya to bed, she will often take her on an imaginative journey into a magical garden. "Instead of reading a story I invite her to close her eyes and relax," says Hilary. To begin, she encourages her daughter to let go of any worries by hanging them on a "worry tree." "I give her some time to do this and you can see from her physiology and her face when she has finished," Hilary explains. She then leads Maya through a lovely garden with colorful flowers and a little stream. Sometimes there will be a guardian angel there waiting to greet her. Hilary makes up the journey as she goes along, and at a certain point leaves her daughter to continue the imaginative adventure for herself. Hilary says that Maya really enjoys this type of guided visualization, and often asks for it. "I can see it calms her down and prepares her for sleep. It helps her feel that everything is OK," says Hilary. "I have also used it, when she was younger, after a temper tantrum. It was a good way of calming her down and reconnecting with herself and with me," she remembers.

Because of their highly developed imaginative abilities, children take very easily to visualization as described by Hilary. Also known as "image work," it is a type of meditation, one that has been used throughout the ages by priests, mystics, and shamans as a creative way of experiencing truths and a form of personal spiritual exercise. Lately it has become a personal growth and healing tool employed by psychologists and psychotherapists. Teachers too use visualization as an aid to creativity in the classroom, and sports psychologists use it to help sports people imagine winning performances.[1]

Children are very good at imagining pictures in their minds. You only have to look at the kaleidoscope of vivid artwork they produce to understand that their heads are full of pictures. Before infants learn to speak, images are a primary way in which they make sense of the world, so it's hardly surprising that mental imagery comes so easily to them. Often this is something that adults lose the ability to create, possibly because it is an activity that is primarily a function of the right-hand side of the brain, the source of creativity. As we develop and pass through the education system, the left-hand side of the brain, home to logic and reason, tends to take over. Unless we use our creative impulses, either in our work or as a means of self-expression in our private time, imagination has a tendency to wither: it's a "use it or lose it" scenario.

Images are not only visual. We can have images of sound, movement, and touch too, although visual images are usually the easiest to conjure up.

HOW DOES VISUALIZATION WORK?

A well-formed image can produce an emotional response and a bodily response. It can also change our behavior. If you are feeling frazzled and stressed, taking a few moments to imagine yourself relaxing on the warm shores of a beach is likely to make you feel calmer, slow your heart rate, and smooth out edgy behavior. It is thought that the power of images lies in their ability to bridge the conscious and the unconscious mind.

For Sigmund Freud, images were the natural language of the unconscious mind, which for the most part he understood as a place where dark, difficult feelings lay repressed. Carl Jung, on the other hand, saw the unconscious as a more light-filled space, containing untapped creativity and spirituality. For Jung, working with images was a way of discovering the hidden treasures that lay deep within us. He was a pioneer with image work, developing a technique called "active imagination," in which clients were encouraged to visualize images and interact with them. This was further expanded upon by the psychologist Roberto Assagioli, who developed psychosynthesis, a psychotherapeutic approach that guides people through places in nature to meet and dialogue with wise spiritual people/beings. Symbolic images are also imagined, like a rose blossoming, to help evoke personal transformation.

HOW TO USE GUIDED VISUALIZATION WITH CHILDREN

There are a number of ways in which you might like to use guided visualization with your child. As they take to it so readily, it's possible to begin this type of inner-world voyaging with children as young as three. Give it a try, and see whether your children are receptive. You will soon be able to judge whether they have enjoyed themselves. Visualization should be a happy way for you to spend time together, so don't force it if they seem reluctant. Giggles and wriggles can all be expected as part of the initial stilling process. Don't get too bothered about this—at least it means they are having a good time. Gently keep them on track and, hopefully, their energy will eventually focus.

Preparation

You need a quiet space, with no distractions. Lighting a candle or dimming the lights may help you symbolically prepare the space. Your child can sit or lie down, as long as she feels comfortable and relaxed. She should close her eyes. To help relax the body you could ask her to tense and relax her body parts, working from her feet upward. You may want to play soft background music.

Tone of voice

Speak in a slow and relaxed voice, pausing regularly to allow time for an image to be fully experienced.

Concluding

Gently bring your child back out of the visualization by asking her to open her eyes, take a few breaths, look around their room and put her feet on the ground or shake her arms and legs. Be available to listen to your child about any of her experiences she may wish to share.

A VISUALIZATION FOR BEDTIME

Here is an example of a type of visualization you can guide your child through to help her relax and sleep. With practice you will be able to make up your own. There are also books available with more suggestions. This visualization is adapted from one written by Maureen Garth.[2]

Above your head is a beautiful star. It is shining down on you with a lovely white light. Can you see the light? It glows onto your face and goes right through your body, through your neck and shoulders, glowing through your heart and stomach, down to your legs and toes. You are filled with a radiant light. You are now about to go into a magical garden. There is a big gate in front of you. Can you see it? I want you to open that gate and step inside. There waiting to greet you is an angel. You are very special to this angel. The angel is a loving friend who will look after you and help you on your journey. Before you go any further into the garden, your angel takes you to a Worry Tree. Here you can hang up any problems or things that you are worrying about. Take a moment to let go of these things . . . When you've finished, follow your angel further into the garden. What do you see there? What color are the flowers? Can you smell them? Look at the trees. Listen out for the sound of a babbling stream. Follow that sound and let it take you to the water. Reach down and touch the cool water with your hand. Now follow your angel further into the garden, and explore together . . .

At this point give your child time to continue the journey in her own imagining. Then bring the visualization to a conclusion.

You are now going to return to the gate through which you entered the garden. Walk past the Worry Tree, remembering to leave your problems hanging there. Say good-bye to your angel, who will always be there for you when you need help. Go out through the gate and gently close it behind you.

VISUALIZATION TO HELP OVERCOME ANXIETY

Inner images can give advice about how to help ourselves during times of need. Dr. Brian Roet, a former GP in Australia, is a hypnotherapist and psychotherapist based in London who for the past ten years has been using visualization to help children overcome emotional problems. He claims a 60 to 70 percent success rate with his child patients, who can be as young as five. "The inner world of children is alive with pictures, often in strange and symbolic forms," he says. "The pictures represent feelings and may be out of date or inappropriate. Often they cause limitations and problems rather than solutions." In his sessions, Dr. Roet encourages children to explore unpleasant feelings and convert them into images. He then invites them to change the image in a way that feels positive. For example, he worked with a nine-year-old girl who was frightened about going to school because of experiences in her past. Dr. Roet asked her to go inside herself and look at her fear. She saw a dragon in her stomach. He encouraged her to go and pat the dragon. After a while the girl began to smile. "We are going to be friends and he's going to come to school and protect me," she told Dr. Roet. Since then the girl has gone to school quite happily.

Dr. Roet says that, with care, parents can also work with their children in this way: it doesn't have to be the preserve of the professional. "There's no magic art to it. It's just guiding someone in without being overly directive. You must use what I call 'clean language,' which means not putting images in there for them," he says. Here are the steps he recommends.

1. Ask about specific feelings that your child finds difficult. Find out where they reside in the body.
2. Ask your child to "go inside" and look at the feeling. Can he describe it to you? Does it have a color and shape; does it represent a person, animal, or mythological figure?
3. Ask your child what he would like to do with the internal picture. How would he like to change it to make it feel better? He may want to change the color, make friends with the animal or person, or make it appear less ferocious.
4. Allow time for him to imagine this and make these changes.
5. Invite your child to open his eyes and come back into the room. Let him share his experiences with you.
6. Support these changes by suggesting he spend a few minutes at bedtime, going back inside to check out the progress.

VISUALIZATIONS BASED ON A SPIRITUAL STORY

A visualization can help a child enter fully into a spiritual story and hear its message. This type of spiritual exercise was recommended by St. Ignatius, the sixteenth-century founder of the Jesuits. Ignatian prayer is a way of using the imagination to experience scripture. After reading a passage in the Bible you imagine yourself to be there at the scene, seeing, hearing, and smelling all the events. You can talk to characters, even Jesus himself, to help understand the passage.

Such techniques can be applied to other spiritual texts too. You may want to work with a children's story, or a folk or fairy tale that expresses spiritual truths. Be careful not to use anything too scary, especially if your child is easily disturbed by such things.

Here are a few guidelines.

1. Read the story to your child first, so he is familiar with it.
2. Invite him to close his eyes and imagine himself to be present during one of the key scenes.
3. Ask him to imagine what it looks like? What can he hear and smell?
4. Suggest that he might like to talk to someone who is there. Who does he choose, and what does he say? What does the person say to him?

Don't try to use visualization as a way of "tricking" your children into a spiritual experience as defined by you. Use open-ended questions as much as possible when exploring meanings, and allow your children to make their own interpretations of what they imagine. You could offer your children this experience as an alternative to a bedtime story or prayer, or as a relaxing way to end their day.

SPIRITUAL PRACTICES FOR PARENTS

Try visualization for yourself. You could work with a story that has spiritual resonance for you, entering deeply into it by imagining yourself present in a key scene. Alternatively, try Dr. Roet's visualization, perhaps to help you deal with an aspect of parenting that you are finding difficult.

16

Get Creative

Our creative dreams and yearnings come from a divine source. As we move toward our dreams, we move toward our divinity.

JULIA CAMERON, *The Artist's Way* [1]

L AST NIGHT TWO of my children enjoyed a spiritual experience of the highest order. It was an encounter with the divine that left them effervescent with joy (and very messy). It required no elaborate religious ritual or holy man. However, I did have to buy white paper, poster paint, and paintbrushes. These new purchases were greeted with such enthusiasm when I got home that within the space of an hour they had produced between them about twenty paintings, and we ran out of space in which to dry them all. Iona, who is three, painted a series of simple faces, and six-year-old Benedict painted houses, cheetahs, and antelopes. A child's poster-paint creations do not appear to be something that we should regard with the sacred reverence reserved for such triumphs as Michelangelo's Sistine Chapel, yet they are an amazing demonstration of our impulse to create. A child will embark on a creative process with all the intensity and absorption of a "professional" artist. The results don't fetch thousands of dollars on the art market, but I personally adore looking at children's artwork, which is often vibrant, spontaneous, and charming. "It took me a whole lifetime to learn to draw like children," said Pablo Picasso.

There is a deep need in us to contribute to God's creation with our own unique creative efforts. In painting we dip our brush into our soul, and do our best to bring into the world what feelings, thoughts, dreams, and mysteries we find there. The same is also true of drawing, writing, playing a musical instrument, and dancing. And it doesn't have to be high brow: growing sweet peas, making a birthday cake, sewing a fancy-dress costume, or building a wooden playhouse are all creative ways in which we celebrate the world around us. Matthew Fox, a visionary Episcopal priest who explores the mystical and creative forces within the Christian tradition, describes creativity as "a place, a space, a gathering, a union, a where—wherein the Divine powers of creativity and the human power of imagination join forces."[2] And you thought the kids were just cutting and pasting!

Children are naturally highly creative. Give them some crayons, a puppet, a silk scarf, or a cardboard box and they will start to imagine things, to fantasize, explore, and experiment. While still young, certainly under seven, children are not encumbered at all by expectations about how their picture should look, or whether they truly have any musical talent on the piano. Creativity is simply a natural process, a joy that needs no judgment. They jump on the creative wave as it approaches, have a great time, and then look around for the next surfing opportunity. As they get older, they become more concerned about how their achievements are evaluated. Is my picture realistic? How many wrong notes did I play? Creativity can be diminished if their confidence is not sustained. If it is nurtured, it can become the habit of a lifetime that, as described by Carl Jung, permits the spirit that moves them to speak out.

HOW TO ENCOURAGE CREATIVITY

Listen to your children and try to find out what creative activities most interest them. You are a significant role model here: if your children see you playing a guitar, drawing a picture, or crafting something out of wood, they are very likely to want to join in.

Your willingness to be creative with them acts as a catalyst for their own creative expression and nourishes them with ideas and inspiration. Expose your children to a rich variety of creative opportunities, and look out for the activities that really seem to make their eyes sparkle and their souls jump for joy.

Art

Art is possibly the easiest and cheapest creative activity to pursue. All you need is some space (the kitchen table is ideal), plain paper, and easily purchased materials like crayons, poster paints, felt tips, and pencils. Encourage your children to make birthday and Christmas cards and party invites. Offer modeling clay for three-dimensional experimentation, and magazines, old greetings cards, scissors, and glue for collage work. You can never have too much paper, and, thankfully, young children aren't that fussy about what they draw on. Save envelopes, scrap paper, and cardboard, and cut it into different shapes for added interest. Let them transform your patio with pavement chalk. Keep your children company as they paint, if they want you to be there, and offer assistance when necessary. Celebrate their pictures by displaying them on your walls. Children's craft activity books, comics, and TV art programs can be good for inspiration if you are all getting stuck for ideas. Older children may enjoy browsing through art books from the library or visiting art galleries.

Music

Start preschoolers off with fun musical activities and games. Banging on saucepans and making shakers are perennial favorites. Fill glass bottles with varying amounts of water to create a simple xylophone (do supervise any activities involving glass). Try games like "Follow My Rhythm," have musical conversations, or do a Native American rain dance. And don't forget the joy of singing together. Listen to music at home with your children and discuss their reaction to it. If you get the opportunity, take them along to child-friendly musical performances.

There is some debate as to the right time for a child to begin formal musical training. Some recommend eight to eleven years, others believe it can be earlier. If children start too young, they may not have the physical ability or concentration to learn and are terminally put off. Good first instruments are the recorder (which is also, mercifully, cheap), the piano, and the violin. Children generally need to be over nine to learn brass instruments, which demand a lot of puff. When looking for your child's first music teacher, focus on how he or she relates to your child, rather than their musical accomplishments. At this young stage children will benefit most from a teacher who can get them excited about their instrument and make it fun.

Drama and dance

Children are constantly on the move, as any tired parent can testify. Jumping, wriggling, and running are all basic necessities to them. From the moment they wake up to the moment they close their eyes, their little bodies are on the go, go, go. Dance and creative movement come very easily to them, and at a young age they do it unself-consciously and with great joy. There are lots of dance and movement games you can play at home together. We often have a family disco in the living room when the children's energy levels are particularly high. Musical statues or musical hugs (where you have to find a partner to hug when the music stops) are easy dance games to have up your sleeve. Give children a scarf or streamers to dance with and they will add lovely imaginative flourishes to their performance. Formal dance lessons, like ballet and tap, can begin with conviction at age seven or eight, but children can have lots of fun from an earlier age. And, as Billy Eliot showed us, it's not just for the girls.

Drama too can easily be part of your family fun. Animal charades is a favorite with young children, and those of all ages can create puppet shows. It's fun to stage dramatic performances for visitors. Get friends and cousins to join in for a larger cast. We did a small Christmas nativity last year, which was a source of great delight for children and grandparents alike. Keep a well-stocked dressing-up box on hand. It doesn't have to be filled with expensive outfits: bargains from charity shops can be cut down, and all manner of outfits can be imagined with a length of cloth.

HOW TO ADD SPIRITUAL DEPTH TO CREATIVITY

As discussed earlier, creativity in itself is a spiritual experience. However, there are ways in which you can make the practice even more nourishing and take its roots deeper down into the soil of the soul. Here are some ideas.

- *Encourage your children to take a short moment of calm before they begin their creative pursuit.* This might take the form of a little prayer or simple breathing exercise. If your children are receptive and willing, taking this moment will help them center before they begin, and allow the creative process to emerge from a more integrated whole self.
- *Invite your children to draw a picture or play a piece of music as part of their nighttime prayer ritual.* They could draw a picture of those things that they want to say thank you to God for, or a picture of those who are in special need of God's love right now. They could choose to play a piece of music that sums up the spirit of the day. Similarly, artwork of food and farming can be placed at the center of the table as an alternative family grace.
- *Use your children's creative work when you hold family rituals.* If you are celebrating spring, this is the time to get your children to paint daffodils or whirl around the house to Vivaldi's *Four Seasons*. If you do follow a religious calendar, use creativity at home to mark its progress, for instance by painting eggs at Easter.
- *Place your children's creative achievements on your home altar.* This lets your children know that their art is worthy of this very special place in the home, and helps them make the connection between their creative life and worship.

- *Suggest children turn a spiritually nourishing story into a play.* With a little encouragement children are often eager to make a story their own by embodying different characters and scenes.
- *Use creative pursuits to ground thoughts and feelings experienced after creative visualization* (see chapter 15). A picture could be drawn to show the beautiful garden which was imagined, or to illustrate a story that was visualized.
- *Encourage your children to express their feelings about nature.* When you go to the park or out into the countryside, take art materials with you so your children can express their experience of nature through images or words (see chapter 25).

When your children's artwork becomes explicitly sacred in this way, be extra mindful about the ways in which you respond to it. Treat it with care and reverence, for it has emerged from a very tender part of their being—their soul. By letting them witness that their soul creations are worthy of your complete, loving attention, you are conveying to your children the powerful message that they matter very much.

HOW TO TALK TO YOUR CHILDREN ABOUT THEIR CREATIVE ACHIEVEMENTS

- *Invite your children to discuss their creations with you.* Give them your attention and explore their thoughts and feelings about their artistic pursuits. This helps them consider their artistic achievements, and also lets them know that you consider them valuable.
- *Focus on the process rather than the product.* The painting before you may not be highly accomplished, since children have often not yet acquired the necessary skills. "I can see you really had fun doing that" or "You were really concentrating" make affirming observations.
- *Use genuine praise.* It's tempting to lavish praise on children no matter what they have done. Praise of course has

its place, but children soon tune into inauthentic admiration. Instead of a hollow "It's wonderful," try going for detail, describing what you see or hear: "You've used lots of lovely bright red in this picture," or "I can hear how hard you have been practicing."

A SPIRITUAL PRACTICE FOR PARENTS

How do you get creative? Make an opportunity to create a piece of artwork to celebrate your children. It may be many years since you last tried drawing a picture, composing a song on the guitar, or writing a poem or prayer. Look at happy photos, trinkets, and memorabilia for inspiration. Don't worry about whether your creation is "good" or "bad" but instead focus on how the process deepens and sharpens your feelings of love for your family.

Be Body Aware

The body is the harp of your soul, And it is yours to bring forth sweet music from it or confused sounds.

KAHLIL GIBRAN, *The Prophet*

BABIES AND CHILDREN love to move. Watch a baby lying on its back and notice how it pedals its legs and grabs its toes purely for pleasure. Older children are in heaven when they can run, jump, skip, swim, and perform all types of acrobatics. Body-awareness comes before language, and is one of a child's first passions. Movement for a child is a necessary expression of the immense inner force of growth energy. Boys in particular, who have 30 percent more muscle bulk than girls, have an urgent need to exercise their bodies, often to the annoyance of adults, who want them to sit still in the classroom or at the dinner table.

The epidemic of childhood obesity sweeping Western nations is a tragic symptom of a lifestyle that has become too sedentary. The reasons for this are well known: outdoor play is restricted because of fears about traffic and child abductions; fewer children walk to school; less time is given to PE in the school timetable; and busy parents may have become overly dependent on television and computer games to entertain their children. This is compounded by a modern diet high in fat. Such a lifestyle makes a child not only physically sluggish, but spiritually apathetic too. The Bible urges, "Glorify God in your body" (1 Corinthians 6:20); there can be little of that going on in an overweight child slumped in front of a television! If children are not getting sufficient exercise, the vital energies that naturally surge through their young bodies stagnate unhealthily, and spiritual growth is stunted. Physical fitness, suppleness, and energy are all God's gifts to children, and as spiritual parents we must provide ample opportunity for them to enjoy what they have been given. This includes teaching them to respect their bodies by encouraging a healthy diet, and structuring their lives with routines of regular rest and exercise.

Many doctors believe that adult lifestyle-related diseases, such as heart disease and obesity, may be prevented if childhood is more active. According to the American Heart Association, children aged five to eighteen need at least one hour a day of moderate activity—such as swimming, brisk walking, cycling, or dancing—supplemented by twice-weekly activities—such as climbing, skipping, jumping, and gymnastics—to enhance muscular strength.

EXERCISE AND SPIRITUALITY

Physical exercise is valued by many spiritual traditions, not only as a means of perfecting the body, but also as a way of perfecting the soul. Philosopher and psychotherapist Eugene Gendlin believes that as we grow up we start to ignore our body as a source of knowledge. We tend to put a lot more energy into our intellect as a way of knowing the world than into our physical interface with it. Gendlin noticed how difficult it was to work with university academics and other clients who are highly trained in the art of thinking. As a consequence he devised a psychotherapeutic practice called "focusing," which helped these clients get in touch with their "felt sense" of a situation. Gendlin believes that children are naturally aware of this felt sense of their bodies, and can lose this ability as they are raised within the academic system.

When this ability is at its height, we can lose ourselves in the moment as we exercise, and feel a tremendous union between mind, body, and spirit. Children are naturally talented at this—

yet another way in which they can enlighten us. My eldest son is particularly fond of running, and it is in those moments when he flies like the wind that I can see he is fully alive and at one with the world.

Any form of physical activity can potentially be a meditation in motion: swinging on the monkey bars in the park, riding a bike, swimming, playing football or tennis. Every child will develop his or her own favorites, given the space and the opportunity. There are, however, only a few sport or fitness activities that explicitly train the participant to treat the exercise as a path to spiritual energy. The greatest holistic exercise systems to emerge have come from India and the Far East, where in yoga and the martial arts there is much wisdom about energy flow in the human body. The Western world has now adopted these exercise systems with enthusiasm. Yoga and martial arts classes abound in the United States; more recently there have been adaptations that are suitable for children. Enrolling your children in one of these classes may be a helpful way for them to maintain that mind, body, spirit connection which at first they find so easy, but which later becomes increasingly difficult as their focus moves toward their intellectual capabilities.

You may already practice yoga or a martial art yourself, in which case you could exercise alongside your children. There are now a number of videos on the market that you might find helpful. Family classes in yoga and the martial arts are also becoming quite popular. I think they are a great idea, particularly for parents who seem to spend far too long waiting around while their offspring engage in interesting after-school activities and get precious little time to do anything for themselves.

YOGA

Yoga originated in India more than 5,000 years ago, and is considered to be a path to enlightenment as well as an excellent way to improve suppleness and strength. It has been extremely popular with adults in the West since the 1960s, and more recently yoga classes, books, and videos[1] have become available for children. Children's yoga classes are commonplace now in most of the major cities in the United States, and are gradually becoming more widespread as the benefits become recognized. The traditional stretching and bending postures have been adapted for children, most commonly by giving them fun animal names with accompanying noises. Not all types of yoga are suitable for children. Ashtanga, for instance, uses breath work that is too demanding for those under fourteen. Pip Acibar is a children's yoga teacher working with children in the UK from four years upward. She uses stories to guide children through the session, taking them on imaginative jungle and farm journeys, where they form the shapes of the animals they encounter. Her sessions always begin with a short guided visualization: the children lie on the floor, eyes closed, and are encouraged to picture a tranquil nature scene. "At first I wasn't sure how this would work, but it's proved to be very successful," she says. "The parents of boys have told me that it is a useful way to help calm them down." The lesson ends with the intonation of sounds, which again she says goes down well with children.

Children's yoga teachers say that the practice, as well as being good for fitness and health (it's particularly helpful for asthma), sharpens a child's ability to focus and helps to develop self-discipline—both essentials for the spiritual path. The meditative aspects of yoga enable children to become aware that they have an internal life, "which really helps children get to know themselves," says Pip.

MARTIAL ARTS

Popular children's television programs like *Power Rangers* and *Teenage Mutant Ninja Turtles* have brought the martial arts into children's awareness. Watching these programs, horrified parents might think that the martial arts were nothing more than an action-packed punch-up. However, in origin they come from Buddhism, Confucianism, and Taoism, and in their fullness are a spiritual discipline as well as a form of self-defense and exercise. Most martial arts originate from Japan, Korea, or China, and there are many different children's classes to choose from, including tae kwon do, aikido, judo, and kung fu. My two boys are learning karate, and I have been much impressed with the discipline, courtesy, and respect that are part of the training. There seems to be a strong sense of morality at work, and my boys take very seriously the instructor's warning that karate should never be used aggressively. At their best the martial arts are a physical and mental discipline, with a good instructor cultivating a particular attitude of awareness, harmony, and nonviolence. There is too a lesson there in toughness that imprints on the mind (making it very beneficial for children who are timid and fearful). It also seems to be a healthy way of channeling that "lion cub" aggression that tends to run riot in boys particularly. T'ai Chi Ch'uan deserves a special mention as the "softest" and most internal of all the martial arts, and regarded by many as an exquisite moving meditation. As with yoga, classes in t'ai chi have been adapted for children using animal movements and games to make it fun.[2]

FAMILY WALKS

It is good to get children into the habit of walking for pleasure. Walking is a much underestimated exercise that can be slipped effortlessly into daily life at no cost, and with no special kit or skills needed. Walking in nature is one of the most popular ways in which we relax and feel connected to creation; it is something that we naturally seem to want to do to calm and renew ourselves. Regular family walks are a wonderful opportunity to spend time together, giving you not only physical benefits but emotional and spiritual ones too. "There's soul in sole": ask Gandhi, Buddha, and Christ, who all did a lot of walking in order to strengthen their spirit.

Walking in nature can be a very mindful exercise, during which we become more aware of our environment and allow ourselves to be touched by its joy. Buddhists practice walking meditations, of which there are two general kinds. Try teaching them to children five years old and upward, keeping the sessions short (not more than a few minutes) and simultaneously engaging in the practice yourself.

Awareness of movement

Focus your awareness on the sensation of walking: the contact of your feet on the ground, the lift and forward motion of the leg. If any other thoughts come into your awareness, gently brush them aside and concentrate once again on your step. It's best not to look at your feet, just keep looking ahead.

Follow the breath

Focus on your breath, inhaling with one step and exhaling on the next. Keep a steady pace and return wandering attention to the breath and your feet.

Christians also use walking as a spiritual practice, sometimes called "prayer walking." Medieval monasteries were designed with large open spaces, explicitly for monks and nuns to engage in walking prayer. It may incorporate a meditative aspect similar to the Buddhist practice, a conversational prayer or a moment of reflection. You could also repeat a short prayer aloud as a mantra. Here are ways to try this with children.

Share spoken prayers

As you walk along as a family, speak aloud any spontaneous prayers that come into your mind. You might want to give thanks for things that you see around you, or pray for the well-being of people you pass or animals you come across, as well as Mother Earth herself.

Reflect on a reading

Read to your children a short reflective piece, or ask a searching question. Hold this in your mind as you walk, and happily share thoughts and ideas as they occur to you.

Chant or sing

Choose a short prayer or affirmation that you can chant together as a mantra while you walk. Or give a rousing family rendition of a song or hymn with meaningful lyrics/words (remote locations may be best for this!).

Children sometimes complain that going for a walk is boring. One of the first moans you might hear is that they are getting tired, but, miraculously, if something interesting comes their way they suddenly spring into life again. Try to ensure family walking is an enjoyable experience by making it as child-friendly as possible. This means keeping walks short and age appropriate. Have plenty of breaks, with little treats to eat and drink along the way. Plan a route with places that will interest them, like rivers, lakes with ducks, playgrounds, a hill where they can fly a kite, a curious landmark. Small reference books can be useful to identify wild birds or flowers. Older children may enjoy learning to map read or follow a compass. Use your imagination to make your surroundings come alive, with fairies in the bluebells and goblins in hollow trees. Engage in a game of chase, a competition of silly walks. Have a scavenger hunt: look for interesting leaves, pebbles, shells, a discarded bird's nest. Be enthusiastic about your walk, and know that it's doing your family soul the power of good, as well as being great for general fitness.

A SPIRITUAL PRACTICE FOR PARENTS

This simple exercise shows how changing our body can also change our state of mind. Spend a few moments clenching your fists as tightly as you can. How does this make you feel? It is likely to make you tense, possibly angry; you may feel that you are struggling and holding on. Now relax and open your hands, holding the palms upward. How does this make you feel? You may find yourself much more relaxed, open, and ready to receive.

18

Enjoy the
Spirit of Play

"But whatever his weight in pounds, shillings, and ounces,
He always seems bigger because of his bounces."

A.A. MILNE, *from Winnie the Pooh's poem about Tigger*

YOU CAN FIND yourself doing some very unexpected things as a parent. My husband John recently enjoyed parading around at one of our son's birthday parties as a clown with a green curly wig. And each Christmas he dresses up as Santa Claus and pays a daytime visit with a present he forgot to leave when he came down the chimney. I have now perfected the art of "silly walks," a game we play when the children have grown tired of walking. And the other day I completely surprised myself by dancing around the living room with yellow streamers, pretending to be a sunbeam.

Children need to play and have fun. It's an essential developmental need, as well as being what they do best. It provides grown-ups with the most wonderful excuse we have to be deliriously silly. As parents we have a sensational opportunity to rediscover that playful, creative part of ourselves that may have got completely squashed by the sobriety of the adult world. With a little person in tow, we can give ourselves permission to let go of the cares and concerns of life, and revel in a moment of carefree silliness. The word "silly" derives from the Germanic *selig*, meaning "blessed," so as you crawl on all fours around the living room braying like a donkey, bear in mind that your frivolity is as lofty as angelic surges of sacred choral music. Many spiritual traditions have their "fool" figures, notably the Sufis of Islam, Christians, Zen Buddhists, and Jews. The fool is also a popular figure in folklore. The Hindus believe that the universe came into being as part of divine play—not the work of God, but the play of God, the Vishnulila (lila meaning "play"). When at his best, the fool is innocent, spontaneous, and joyful, and has a wisdom that others have forgotten.

Having fun as a family has another important function: it bonds us. We fall in love with each other when we play together. There are few parental experiences that are more delightful than creating with your children a symphony of giggles, chortles, and belly laughs. Freeze-frame those moments and really allow them to enter you. Such moments will become snapshots that record some of the happiest moments in your photo album of life. The well-known spiritual writer David Spangler says that he does not let a day go past without telling his children that he loves them and making them laugh or sing a song.[1] That is good advice for us all.

TURN EVERYDAY ACTIVITIES INTO PLAY

A parent I know remembers how as a child his father made him sweep the leaves off the grass at the weekend. It was a boring and miserable chore, where the emphasis was on joylessly getting every single leaf swept away. "My father would shout at me if I left any leaves on the grass," he remembers. Now, as an adult, he has decided to take a very different approach with his own children. "We make sweeping the leaves fun. I get my girls to race each other and see who can get the largest pile. We make a family game of it. We throw a few leaves around, and I certainly don't get annoyed with them if there are a few left scattered about." There's an important lesson in this leaf-sweeping story. If we can find our inner joy and sense of playfulness, even the most mundane and unpleasant tasks can become a pleasure. It takes very little to tip a child's experience over into merriment: a silly face, a raspberry noise, a challenge, a funny voice or song can all be the sugar that helps the medicine go down. I sometimes turn into the "Mommy Monster" when I want the children to tidy their rooms. I snort and roar at the bottom of the stairs, counting down the seconds before I ascend and gobble up any children who still haven't put all their toys away. There are squeals of excited delight upstairs as they toss all the Lego back in the box. There are of course also days when I feel too tired and ratty to play the fool and shout bad-tempered orders instead. I know from experience that this approach is much less effective, and leaves everyone feeling down. As parents we need to contact our playful, joyful spirit as often as we can, and there's no better way to practice this than by starting with the everyday business of life.

VACATIONS AND DAYS OFF

Vacations often stand out in our childhood memories. These happy, carefree recollections, set apart from daily life, are the ones that seem to make the strongest imprint on our young minds. I can still remember eating cockles in Cornwall, UK, hearing the unfamiliar sound of seagulls when I woke up in the morning, and crying in the car because I didn't want to go back home. I would have been about three years old.

When we go away we have the opportunity to experience life differently. From a spiritual perspective, think of your family vacations not as an escape but as an arriving. If you have been living in a flat and meaningless way, this may be the antidote that you all need. Don't take just your bodies on vacation; take your family soul too. We so rarely have time to take in the riches of life, or, as Saint Ignatius says, "to taste them in their profundity and make them part of ourselves." Conceptualize your vacation as something of a pilgrimage. This is a journey that is made within many spiritual traditions: Aboriginal young men go on walkabout, Christians travel to the Holy Land or the shrines of saints, and for Muslims there is the Hajj. The purpose is always to feel ourselves moving closer to God. In the words of theologian Marcus Borg, [2] a pilgrimage "expresses the yearning of the heart to be in the presence of God; because during pilgrimage the self is pointed toward its destination. It is a physical embodiment of inclining the heart toward God." A good holiday will leave everyone feeling flushed, and renewed by God's grace.

TEN VERY SILLY GAMES TO PLAY WITH YOUR CHILDREN BEFORE THEY GROW UP

1. The traditional toe game "This little piggy went to market," accompanied by lots of tickles.
2. Splash tag. An outdoor game of tag in which the person who is "it" tries to catch others by hitting them with a wet sponge.
3. Have a competition in which you try to balance either a ball or a broomstick on your finger.
4. Blow up several balloons and together try to keep them all afloat in the room. The more balloons you inflate, the sillier it gets.
5. Have a silly tongue twister competition.
6. Apple bobbing. Float apples in large bowl of water and attempt to get them out using only your mouth.
7. Knock your socks off. A wrestling game in which you attempt to get your opponent's socks off.
8. Paint a clown's face on each other, or give each other shaving-foam beards.
9. Make crazy hats to wear for dinner. You can create some wild ones with modeling balloons.
10. Jump waves together at the beach.

Vacations don't have to be expensive or exotic to be a tremendous pilgrimage for children. A special day out can offer plenty of jump-up-and-down excitement. Many of the spiritually minded parents I know swear by camping, and can talk lyrically at length about the joys of immersing themselves in nature and living a basic outdoor life for a few days or weeks each summer. Putting watches away and living by the natural rhythms of the day is a liberation.[3] And there is much to be said for days off from school doing nothing much at all: making mud pies, swinging on an old rope across a river, hunting for seashells, and playing Pooh sticks. Children, whose modern lives can sometimes be desperately over-scheduled, are often crying out for slow outdoor living such as this.

Enjoy your vacations together. Sure, the kids might throw up in the car or argue over beds, and there will always be a pile of laundry to do when you get home, but vacations are also a distinctive time in which God's generosity and abundance may be particularly apparent. Seize the opportunity to cultivate your inner joy during vacation time, and watch the harvest you will reap with your children.

Practice Loving
Family Discipline

A river with no banks is a big puddle.

UNKNOWN

DISCIPLINE. IT HAS become a difficult word in child rearing, hasn't it? I thought long and hard over whether I would use it in the title of this chapter, because for many of us it conjures up harsh images of the "spare the rod, spoil the child" type. This kind of child discipline is something that we hopefully left behind in the Victorian era, when hearts were hardened by a culture in which upper lips had to be stiff and corsets had to be rigid. The liberal, permissive 1960s changed child-rearing philosophy forever, and today many of us deplore corporal punishment and the notion that children should be seen and not heard. But I think the word deserves a second chance. In its origins "discipline" comes from the Latin word for "instruction," and a "disciple" is a student under the leadership of a teacher. For me, child discipline is more about training than punishment; used wisely it is guidance to ensure that children become the best human beings they can be. It aims to cultivate all that is benevolent in a child's nature and discourage any malevolent traits.

Without discipline children may find it hard to exercise self-control and tell right from wrong; they may feel anxious and lost because they are not cradled by safe boundaries, and ultimately they struggle to fit in socially.

Even the most angelic children will misbehave at times. Naughtiness in children is something that no parent can avoid, and a certain amount of it is normal. It's a healthy sign that your children are testing out their power in the world and learning about the limits of acceptable behavior. It may also be a way to seek attention (more love, in other words), or a response to a stressful situation. Having to discipline a child is one of the most challenging tasks a parent faces. The misbehavior can make us feel angry, and often we flounder around for effective strategies. Our children may become hostile toward us, and we can find ourselves in hot dispute. "Discipline, to be sure, is never pleasant; at times it seems painful, but afterward those who have been trained by it reap the harvest of a peaceful and upright life," according to biblical scripture (Hebrews 12:11). Remember, your ultimate intention is to instill in your children self-discipline, a sense of personal responsibility, and an ability to make moral choices.

SET UP FAMILY RULES

Setting up family ground rules, to which everyone is committed, is an excellent way to achieve a "peaceful and upright" life together. The ground rules give a family what walls give a house: support, boundaries, and security. Many schools today have ground rules (they're cheerfully called "golden rules" at my children's schools). All religious communities have rules, obedience to which is seen as a spiritual discipline. The right rules turn a house into a home, in which children can feel respected and safe.

SPIRITUAL WISDOM AND CHILD DISCIPLINE

So how do we encourage our children to adhere to the family ground rules, and what do we do when they are broken? In our secular society spiritual wisdom is rarely considered when we are trying to work out how best to tackle these parenting issues.

There aren't many signs on the journey but, as a start, I offer the following ideas.

TOP TIPS FOR SETTING UP FAMILY GROUND RULES

➤ Come up with your ground rules together. Brainstorm ideas, and make sure everyone has a say.

➤ Aim to have no more than five or six ground rules—you don't want to overwhelm your children with too many. Choose the rules that seem to be most important at the time.

➤ Frame your ground rules positively, by describing the behavior you want. For example, "no hitting" becomes "we work out conflict by talking and listening." If you do choose to include the no's, make sure you balance them with positive options too.

➤ Write your ground rules down on a large piece of paper and display them somewhere in your home. Your children could illustrate the notice with relevant pictures.

➤ Reassess your ground rules regularly. There may be times when changes need to be made.

Love will always help

If you believe love to be the supreme unifying principle of life, then love has to play the starring role in the way you discipline your children. Love and affection is the strongest, most potent energy available to us as parents. There is no behavioral problem that cannot be improved by our love.

So what does this love look like? How does it work in practice? First, of course, there has to be affection. A loving discipline system is rooted in a relationship with your child that is tender: you spend plenty of time together hugging, kissing, holding hands, offering your lap, and cuddling. Make a time every day when you are physically close to your child. Tell your daughter frequently

that you love her, and that you always will, even if you are some-times annoyed at something she has said or done. Let your son know that your love for him is not dependent on whether he does well in a test at school, manages to score a goal at football or gets to sing the solo in the school choir. You love him no matter what. He's fantastic just as he is. When a child has done wrong, disapprove of the behavior but still love the child. In so doing, we need to be mindful of our language. "You're a silly boy" labels and condemns the child. "That was a silly thing you did," condemns only the behavior.

There will be times when this type of love seems to gush out of us freely, without any effort on our behalf. And then there will be times when our child has misbehaved and angered us, when we lose touch with these feelings. This is when we remember a nugget of wisdom from the well-known spiritual writer M. Scott Peck: "Love is an act of will—namely an intention and an action. Will also implies choice. We do not have to love. We choose to love."[1]

It is at these moments that we choose to love our children by practicing empathy, deep listening without judgment. There are a number of techniques, which we can all learn, that help us show empathy. We can sit quietly, listening without interruption or criticism. We can reflect back what has just been said to show that it has been heard. But for real empathy to occur, there has to be authentic heart connection. We need to have a soft heart to demonstrate real empathy, and this can be very difficult if we are feeling angry. I know I have practiced this "empty empathy" many times, going through the listening techniques that I know I should be using, but not really seeing into my child's heart because mine was too hardened. If parents are to lovingly discipline children, we may first need to do a little work on our own hearts. We need to become aware of any hard shell that surrounds it, and do our best to crack it open. We can do this by trying to separate the child from the behavior. A moment of prayer may help. A short meditation practice may work. You could use visualization, perhaps conjuring up images of times when you did feel very loving with your child. Some people may find that a burst of physical activity releases angry feelings. See what works for you.

If you can get to the position where you are able to listen to your children with real empathy, together you are in a space where transformation is possible. First, your children will know that they are valuable, they are not alone, and there is a way out of the rut of trouble into which they have dug themselves. In the words of the writer Stephen R. Covey, "Instead of wasting their energy defending themselves, they're able to focus on interacting with their own conscience and unleashing their growth potential."

Feed the good wolf

A Native American grandfather was talking to his grandson. He said, "I feel as if I have two wolves fighting in my heart. One wolf is the vengeful, angry, violent one. The other wolf is the loving, compassionate one." The grandson asked him, "Which wolf will win the fight in your heart?" And the grandfather reflected for a while and answered, "The one I feed." One of the best ways to encourage positive behavior in children is through praise. Often we put far more energy into telling them off about the things they have done wrong than praising them for the things they are getting right. I know that when my children fight, I rush into the room yelling at them to stop, but I often forget to rush in to tell them how peaceful and friendly they are being when playing cooperatively together. It's easy to forget, but when I have tried the latter tactics they have worked, almost miraculously. It's important to remember to tell our children how pleased we are when they show good manners at the table, share sweets with a friend, clean their room, or diligently get on with their homework.

Name your children's virtues frequently. From a spiritual perspective, virtues like kindness, patience, courage, generosity, and honesty come from the soul. They are inner gifts and are universally valued by all faiths. Get into the habit of describing the virtuous behavior that you want, rather than the bad behavior that you don't: for example, "Please be considerate," rather than "stop bothering me." These tactics are hard to remember, I know, especially when you are busy and tired, but as parents we need to do our best to feed and nurture the good wolf at every opportunity.

Find the Middle Way

One of the main struggles facing parents today when considering child discipline is getting the balance right. If parents are too authoritarian, they may dominate children and break their spirit, or cause them to rebel. If parents are too permissive, children may become unruly, selfish, spoiled, and impulsive. It can be a cause of conflict between the adult generations too. The Buddhist precept of "seeking the Middle Way" is useful here. According to Buddhist teachings, Siddhartha Gautama, the Buddha, was born into a royal family of great privilege. When he ventured outside the walls of his palace he was confronted by human suffering for the first time and was appalled. In response he became a homeless holy man, leading a life of strict self-denial for six years. This didn't lead to the happiness he hoped, and instead he abandoned it for the Middle Way. This was a path of neither pampered luxury nor self-denying poverty, and it eventually led to his enlightenment. It's a useful model to bear in mind when trying to steer a course between "No! Because I said so . . ." and "Whatever you want, whenever you want it, sweetheart."

Similar can ideas be found in Taoist thinking, where yin and yang express the balance between two equal and complementary forces.[2] According to Taoists we all know deep inside ourselves where the healthy point of balance is between two fundamental forces; it's something we can intuitively sense, feel, and understand. When you are trying to find the right path, or get the right balance in a situation of conflict between yourself and your child, close your eyes and let your intuition speak. What is it telling you? Where is the healthy point of balance in this situation?

Seek reparation

Reparation is a spiritual principle that holds that good can come out of bad when amends are made, when a bad act is counterbalanced by a good deed. When your child has done wrong, first, talk about it. Let your child know if you feel angry, hurt, or disappointed in her behavior (remember, it's the behavior, not the person). Seize the opportunity to explain why the behavior is wrong, and help your child understand its moral implications. Ask your child why she has behaved in this way, and listen empathetically to the answer. Be fair with your child: you are her role model of how justice should operate.

Your discipline will be most educative if it is in the form of restorative rather than retributive justice—in other words, you give your child the chance to make amends by choosing a punishment for her that fits the crime. For instance, if she deliberately throws food she has to clean up the mess, or if she breaks a window she has to pay for it from pocket money earned by doing extra chores. Your punishment shouldn't be about making your child feel bad about herself, but about creating an opportunity for doing good. It isn't always easy in the moment to think of something that runs exactly counter to the misdemeanor. Time out to "think about it" can be useful, for it gives everyone a chance to cool down. During this time you could ask your child to brainstorm a few ideas about how she can make up for what she has done. If at the end of it all you get a sincere apology, this is a great triumph, and a real sign that your child has learned a lesson and grown spiritually.

Seek reconciliation

For a spiritually minded parent, discipline does not end here. In the Bible the father welcomed back the prodigal son with open arms. We all deserve a second, third, and even fortieth chance. Don't let bad feelings linger in your household. Show tenderness and forgiveness to your child sooner rather than later, in remembrance of the first wisdom "love will always help." As much energy needs to be invested in restoring family harmony as it did in administering appropriate punishment. This is the time for cuddles on the sofa and little chats about what has just gone on. With good listening and empathy, this may be the moment when you get to the root of the problem. This may be when you discover that the school uniform was deliberately scribbled on in felt tip because your child is miserable in class. This may be when you discover that your child kicked his sibling because he needs more reassurance that your love for him is not diminished by the existence of his brothers and sisters. If you practice prayer with your child, inner learning is deepened if he can also feel reconciled with his innermost self, God. Gently encourage him to say sorry during prayers, and thank God that he has the ability to learn from his mistakes and is such a fine child.

LOSING OUR TEMPER

I thought myself to be a very easygoing person until I had children. Now, after a long, tiring, sometimes lonely day with three children, I realize that I can become a monster. No one teaches us as much about our limitations and capacity for anger as children. "The greatest advantage of not having children must be that you can go on believing that you are a nice person. Once you have children you realize how wars start," said the novelist Fay Weldon. All parents lose their tempers sometimes, and say things that they regret and do things that later they wish they hadn't. I interviewed a mother who lives in a spiritual community that throbs with the virtues of love and kindness; she told me that, even there, she didn't know of another mother who hadn't smacked her child or handled him roughly, out of frustration. I have to confess to being secretly pleased about such revelations, because it means that I am no worse than everyone else. However, I still feel intense shame when I realize I am capable of experiencing feelings of violence toward my children. It is a very human and understandable thing, but it makes me feel wounded and lodges painfully in my conscience. I know that at such times I have fallen from grace.

It may be that when we lose our temper we enter a tender, weak part of ourselves that still bears bruises from our own childhood. Our offspring seem to have an inbuilt ability to find these old injuries and give them a sharp poke! You really get to know yourself, bruises and all, when you become a parent.

How to stay cool

When we feel that our temper is about to vent itself, we face two challenges. The first is recognizing that an explosion is imminent. We need to know when we have reached our limit as a parent. The second challenge is to be able to release that anger without reenacting a scene from *The Exorcist*, tempting though that might be. We are a lot more powerful than our children, and an outpouring of uncontrolled anger can be a terrifying experience for them. It may be that we need to remove ourselves from our child for a short period, if this is safe. Go and hit pillows on the bed if necessary—it will really help release tension. Now breathe deeply and visualize a peaceful scene. You could ask God to help you deal with these turbulent feelings, and let the divine healing energy enter you.

Too late?

Maybe we have smacked or shaken our child, called her a nasty name, shouted in her face. It may have felt an ugly relief at the time, but it has left us shriveled by guilt at the sight of the weeping little girl before us. Now we face three different challenges. The first is to say "sorry." This demands humility: we are not perfect, and have more to learn. Children can discover the power of apology from our example: if we can humble ourselves by saying "I'm very sorry, I shouldn't have done that," then so can they.

The next challenge we face is the recognition that we are in need of healing. It may be that we urgently need some time away from the kids: an escape from home may be exactly what will bring us back home. It may be that we need to get extra support, either practically or emotionally. Close your eyes and ask yourself, "What is it that I need? What will help me?"

Finally, we face the challenge of self-forgiveness. This is a good opportunity to pray for ourselves as parents (see Chapter 6), and in so doing we may feel a restored grace enter into the deepest parts of our being. There will be no conclusion to the episode unless we can find in ourselves enough compassion to set in place the things that we need, let go of our feelings of guilt, and move on with faith that things can be better.

SPIRITUAL PRACTICE FOR PARENTS

➤ When feeling stressed, try this simple breathing exercise:
➤ Take a deep breath, and as you slowly breathe out, let go of all your angry feelings.
➤ Take another breath, and this time use it to center yourself in the here and now.
➤ Take a third slow breath, and in so doing ask yourself "What now?"

A HOME
WITH SPIRIT

Make a Sacred Space in Your Home

You must have a room or a certain hour of the day or so where you do not know what is in the morning paper. A place where you can simply experience and bring forth what you are and what you might be. At first you may think nothing's happening. But if you have a sacred space and take advantage of it and use it everyday, something will happen.

JOSEPH CAMPBELL

STONEHENGE IN WILTSHIRE is one of Britain's greatest ancient sacred monuments, dating back more than 4,000 years. The building of it is an astonishing testament to humankind's determination to create sacred space. Experts believe that prehistoric people dragged 4-ton stones all the way from Wales, some 300 miles off, to erect this monument, which may have been used to worship the sun. All they had was their hands, rollers, sledges, and, presumably, an enormous conviction to build a special place that would help them understand the world. It took them 500 years, and the site is still used today by druids to celebrate the summer solstice.

Later generations have toiled over the construction of mosques with domed roofs, and cathedrals with towering spires. These architectural achievements bear witness to the deep yearnings we have for holy space.

Unless you belong to an organized religion, you are unlikely to have a dedicated holy space in your life. It is said that nature is the ultimate location when we are searching for God, and for many of us this is indeed the very best place to be. But there can also be times when we feel the need to home in and find a smaller, more focused spiritual spot.

The home altar, or shrine, can be found in many cultures. Hindus have a household shrine with images of deities, flowers, fruits, and incense. Mexican Catholics have colorful images of Jesus, Mary, and various saints, alongside candles, photos of deceased loved ones, trinkets, and dolls. Even the humblest homes in Bhutan have a Buddhist prayer room. All serve to transform the ordinary into a special place of worship.

Western culture doesn't have this tradition of home altars, although frequently we create them unconsciously. The mantelpiece above the hearth, the heart of the home, is often the place where we put candles, photographs, and decorative objects that mean something to us. Table decorations, especially candles and flowers, are another way in which we symbolically transform a dining room table into an altar.

WHY HOME ALTARS NURTURE A FAMILY'S SPIRIT

- ❧ *Home altars provide private space.* Many of us lack private space in the home, especially if we are one of a couple and don't have our own bedroom. A home altar can be a space to go to when you seek solitude.
- ❧ *Home altars provide sacred space.* They are conducive to prayer, meditation, and family ritual.
- ❧ *Home altars bring nature indoors.* Objects from nature placed on your altar are a helpful reminder of the created world to which you belong.
- ❧ *Home altars can be used to celebrate the seasons and religious festivals.* You can mark the passing year with seasonal items and religious symbols.
- ❧ *Home altars are a focus for inspiration.* When visiting your altar you can read from a spiritual text you find inspiring. Or you can take a card from one of the growing number of spiritual card packs that are available.
- ❧ *Home altars are a place to honor deceased loved ones.* Photos and mementos of those who have died can be treasured here.

> *Home altars can be used to mark family achievements and milestones.* Objects that connect you to important family moments can be placed on your altar to enable contemplation and thanks.
> *Home altars encourage creativity.* It can be after a period of contemplation that we feel most creative. Keep pens and paper handy.
> *Home altars give us a place where we can ask for help and guidance.* Use your altar to help you work through personal struggles, arguments, and pain. Offer them up for help, if this fits into your belief system.

WHOSE ALTAR?

You may want to create an altar that is intended to be used by all family members. In addition, or alternatively, you may prefer a private altar. Hilary and her husband Alvin, who run Words of Discovery, a mail-order company specializing in holistic books for children, have an altar each. Hers is an indoor water feature, his is a Buddhist-style shrine. Jaki lives in a house big enough to have a dedicated meditation room that can be used by all the family. "Whenever my sons naturally need any quiet time they just go there," she says. "We have a Buddha figure in there, a Tibetan singing bowl, incense, and crystals. There are shawls to wrap themselves in and candles. They have to take their shoes off and be quiet there."

Her eldest son, who is eleven, has created a little shrine in his bedroom. It contains crystals and incense, favorite marbles, things he's picked up on walks, and two painted elephants. My family doesn't have a dedicated altar area at present, but we do create a special candle centerpiece decorated with seasonal objects that can be moved around the home according to our needs.

HOW TO BUILD AN ALTAR

First you need to find a space. If you are very lucky you may have a spare room you can devote to the purpose. It may for instance be a far better way of using a spare bedroom. If your home is on a more modest scale, you will instead have to find a suitable corner, windowsill, bedside cabinet, wall shelf. If you have no space at all, you could stow your altar away in a cupboard on a tray that you can lift out. If you are happy to pray around a table, your altar can be as simple as a special table centerpiece. Don't forget the yard or garden too. There are no rules saying a home altar has to be indoors.

OBJECTS TO PUT ON YOUR ALTAR

➤ Religious items such as images of deities, prayer beads, prayer flags
➤ Religious texts, inspirational quotations, spiritual card packs
➤ Plants and flowers
➤ Bells, chimes, a drum, wind chimes
➤ Twigs, leaves, fir cones
➤ Artwork (including the children's)
➤ A water feature
➤ Photographs of loved ones or favorite places
➤ Polished stones and gems
➤ Pebbles and stones gathered on memorable occasions
➤ Essential oils and incense
➤ Candles

Take a moment to tune into the space and bless it, if this feels right. Collect items that you want to place on your altar. This can be an enjoyable shared family activity if the altar is for everyone. All these items should have a deep meaning for you, or one of your family members. Consider objects that appeal to our different senses, including objects you can touch and handle. Children especially may enjoy this. You will also need to be able to sit comfortably, either on chairs or floor cushions.

Don't forget to dust and maintain your altar. This need not be a tiresome chore, but part of a prayer in action.

Altars can be as simple or as elaborate as you want. Those busy Mexican home altars are just as much an expression of God as an altar inspired by Zen minimalism. You can change your altar too, perhaps to mark the seasons or a religious calendar, if you follow one. See your altar as a living creation that echoes both the world around your family and the world within.[1]

Choose Toys
with Care

"Real isn't how you are made," said the Skin Horse. "It's a thing that happens to you. When a child loves you for a long, long time, not just to play with, but REALLY loves you, then you become Real."

MARGERY WILLIAMS, *The Velveteen Rabbit*

IN TODAY'S WORLD it is extremely difficult to control the toys that come into your children's life. The reasons for this are wide ranging, but an underlying factor is that there is a huge array of playthings around and middle-income families have the disposable income to purchase them. The choice of toys available has never been so vast, and the relatively low cost of mass-produced toys means that Santa, friends, and family can afford to be extra generous each year. Children no longer hang up little stockings on Christmas eve, but enormous sacks. Children's birthday parties are now an expected part of the social calendar, and with them arrive a mound of presents to be incorporated into already heaving toy boxes. Then there are those free toys slipped into fast food combo meals, plastic trinkets in cereal boxes, and gifts attached to comics. Huge cavernous warehouses have sprung up all over the country to accommodate the ever-growing range of toys on offer, which somehow cascade into our children's lives like confetti.

The modern toy industry is intricately entwined with film and television. Character toys accompany all Walt Disney releases, and inevitably every popular children's TV show has its merchandise alongside. Toys have become very cartoon-like in appearance and often are literally animated by battery-powered movement and noise. Ads for toys on television appeal directly to children, who from a very early age become accomplished consumers, telling mom or dad exactly what they want. And once you've bought one item, you may be pressured to go on to buy the whole set, because modern toys often come in collections with many add-ons.

But how many of these toys spiritually nourish our children? Is this apparent feast of toys really a famine? The problem with evaluating toys is that there are no easy answers. It's not a science, so you cannot say with certainty that a particular type of toy is the direct cause of a particular type of behavior. Does Barbie really cause anorexia? Is that Power Ranger figure the reason why there was a fight in the playground today? And there's not only the toy to consider; there's also the culture within that the child is playing and the unique personality of the young owner.

Natural toys

Some parents believe there are spiritual values to be found in what have been loosely termed "natural toys," which have a small market niche in the United States thanks largely to specialist toy shops and mail-order catalogues. Natural toys are made from wood and organic fibers, and may even be handmade: these factors combine to make them "living" in a way that molded plastic in primary colors never can. It's cheering to contemplate that such toys may have been made and sold by people who genuinely care about children and their development, rather than mass-produced by companies out to make fast money. "I don't allow my son to play with plastic toys, only wooden ones. I don't like all these plastic, noisy toys. I think they are very confusing," says Annette, the mother of eight-month-old Josiah. It is a hardline that has led to conflict. "I have a friend who kept buying Josiah all these plastic toys. At first I told her to keep them at her house, but then there were so many of them she wanted me to take them home. I had to tell her that I didn't want them. She was very angry at first, but we talked about it and now she chooses wooden gifts. It was very difficult but I felt I had to make a stand."

The natural toy philosophy can be traced back to Rudolf Steiner, the Austrian philosopher and educator, who championed simple, handmade folk toys. He suggested that toys should be "open-ended," that is, not overly detailed, so that there is space for children to fill in the gaps with their own imagination. The face on a Rudolf Steiner-style doll is simple so that children can put in the missing characteristics for themselves. This school of thought would maintain that a battery-operated toy is not the best choice because it does all the work for the child, and the play that it provides is limited and predetermined.

In an ideal world I might have surrounded my children from birth with nothing but natural, handmade wooden toys. They appear to have true educational value; they appeal to my sense of romance about childhood; I find them aesthetically beautiful, and they have an enduring, timeless quality that would inspire me as a parent to care for them properly and urge the children to do likewise. However, I do wonder whether this preference is born out of my fashion sensibilities, rather than an expression of the true needs of my children. It's also hard to stick to the natural-toy position in the face of modern commercialization. Mass-produced toys are cheaper and much more widely available. Although we have some handsome wooden toys at home, we also have a lot of trashy, plastic ones. My children often seem to prefer the latter. They have arrived in our home as gifts, as swaps made at school, as treasures picked up by feverish small hands at fund-raising toy fairs. Sometimes I have given in to pester power because I felt too exhausted to think of a creative alternative. Sometimes it simply felt too mean to refuse to buy the one Christmas present they were begging Santa to bring. Sometimes I could see that ownership of a popular toy would give my child a stronger sense of membership within his peer group.

We have a Barbie at home, we have aggressive action figures and superhero dressing-up clothes. On a bad day it seems as if the worst aspects of our society are being played out in the children's toy collection. To have stopped this invasion I probably would have needed to educate my children at home, take a sledgehammer to the television, and allowed my children to play only with the children of like-minded parents. That is an option that some parents might go for. But if I had kept saying "no," and sending back gifts my children adored, I probably would have ended up with very resentful children who crave the "forbidden fruit" even more. I suppose I have tried to tread a middle path, with varying degrees of success.

Aggressive toys

I have found it particularly difficult to encourage my boys not to choose aggressive fighting toys. I was delighted when my son asked for a farm for Christmas, but was later dismayed to find him enacting a war on it, using the pigs as soldiers!

But maybe I need not feel so concerned about this type of play. Perhaps it is in reality very healthy. It's known that boys engage in more rough and tumble play than girls, and that they may be biologically programmed to engage in energetic, forceful games. "Anything that children do as often and as universally as power play must have some basis in children's development," argues Kathy Reschke, a child development expert with the National Network for Child Care based at Iowa State University. "If children between four and six years old consistently act out dramatic play scenarios that involve power, aggression, and good versus evil, regardless of where they live, economic status, or family background, there must be something that they have in common that is motivating this kind of play." She suggests that children of this age are beginning to understand a morality, a universal code of right and wrong, and that power play is a way for them to grapple with these concepts. Children of this age have very little control over their lives, but in fighting play they create a safe space to experience feelings of being in charge.

We may be wrong in taking the moral high ground with boys and adopting a zero tolerance strategy to fighting play and guns. This is the view of Penny Holland, senior lecturer in early childhood studies at London Metropolitan University, who has studied boys' behavior in preschool settings. She also thinks that weapons and superhero play represent a developmental need for boys. What's more, she argues, if they are constantly receiving negative messages about their chosen games, they absorb the sense that they are bad boys. If left to play as they wish, boys in nurseries often agree rules between themselves to ensure that no one gets hurt. Holland additionally claims that there is scant research to show that early play with toy guns and weapons and superhero-reflective play cause aggressive behavior.

It may be healthy and normal for boys to want to play fight, but guns and many other aggressive toys are a pernicious cultural expression of this need. I know that many parents feel worried by them, as indeed am I.

Where you stand on the superhero play issue eventually is a personal decision: I have settled with the conclusion that it is acceptable for my children to have some fighting toys, but it also important for them to have a wide range of other more open-ended playthings, plus guidance in how they can move beyond the violent good guy/bad guy dramas.

How to choose

So what do we do about choosing toys for our children? Ultimately, parents have to go with their instincts and a great deal of common sense. There are also a few practical questions that you can ask:

- ❧ Is the toy age-appropriate?
- ❧ Is it safe and tough enough to withstand the vigor of play?
- ❧ What will my child learn from this toy?
- ❧ What will it add to my child's toy collection?
- ❧ Does it leave room for my child to play with it imaginatively?

How to avoid toys you don't like

If you feel pressured into buying toys you don't like, there are a few strategies that might help:

- First, you might want to consider that just because you don't like a toy it doesn't necessarily mean it's wrong for your child.
- Don't shame your child about his choice of toy. You will give the message that he must hide his interests, and his confidence could be undermined.
- Show him alternatives. Go to quality toy shops (or let him choose from mail-order catalogues).
- Help your child have a sense of self-worth that does not depend on what toy he has or what the "popular" children are playing with.
- Show him new ways of playing with the action toys he might already have. They could be involved in a rescue mission, or the good guys and bad guys could work together on something.
- There may be times when you just have to say "no." Try to involve your child in this decision by talking with him and explaining why you don't like the toy. Be prepared for him to feel angry. Be empathetic about how he feels.

Don't forget homemade toys

It's a long-standing joke that children get more fun from the cardboard box than the toy it contained. A cardboard box presents a child with endless possibilities. Is it a boat? Or a rocket to the moon? Or a cave for a bear to sleep in? You can paint and decorate a box. Homemade toys allow children to use their imagination, and teach them craft and practical skills. Creating and playing with such toys is also a very enjoyable and meaningful way to spend time together.

A SPIRITUAL PRACTICE FOR PARENTS

If you are unsure about a toy, try this reflective meditation, suggested by author David Carroll.[1]

Stand in front of the object for a moment or two, then close your eyes and try to sense it from the inside. Let it speak to you. Hear its message. The toy in question was conceived by human thought, designed by human intelligence, and built by human contrivance. During its construction something of its creator was put into it, something of the designer's thoughts and emotions. This is the message you're listening for now.

Consider Your Family's Media Habits

I find television very educational. Every time someone switches it on, I go
into another room and read a good book.

GROUCHO MARX

TWO YEARS AGO my household gave up television for Lent.
To put a less puritanical spin on it, we decided that for forty
days and forty nights we would use our usual TV time to do
something different instead. Serendipity had its place in this: our
television suddenly broke down on Ash Wednesday, just as we
were trying to decide what we would do to make Lent a special
time of spiritual observance. So instead of the traditional
Christian fasting and penance, we had instead a motionless, silent
blank screen in the corner of our living room. It would prove to
be a thought-provoking family experiment, leading us to reassess
the place of the television in our home.

If spiritual values are important to you, you may be concerned
about the influence of television on your children. As I am. Is it
harmful? We knew where we stood when it was just *Sesame Street*
and *The Electric Company*, but today it is hard for a parent to keep
track of their children's viewing, which on average in the United
States comes to three-and-half hours a day. We are advised cheerfully that we should sit down and watch television with our off-

spring. This well-intentioned guidance does nothing other than instill guilt, because, as every busy parent knows, a child's viewing time gives you that crucial "get things done" window. What's more, 20 percent of American children aged two to seven have a television in their bedroom. This rises to nearly 50 percent by the time they are eight years old. To a certain extent we have trusted the broadcasters, but that is an assurance that many believe is now misplaced, given the nature of the programs being scheduled. There are several areas of concern.

TV VIOLENCE

I am particularly dismayed at the proliferation of aggressive cartoons in the schedules. Just flipping through the channels makes it clear that children's television is dominated by violent cartoons rather than educational programs. Many people blame cartoons for the increase in aggressive behavior of children in school. These are of course anecdotal comments, and although there is no definitive research to prove clearly that viewing violence on television will lead a child into violent behavior, there is enough evidence to suggest that too much exposure to violence is not a good thing. According to the Child Development Institute, violence on TV makes children less sensitive to the pain and suffering of others; they may become more fearful of the world around them; they may be more likely to behave in an aggressive manner; and they get an unrealistic sense of the amount of true violence that exists in the world.

Yet children are often drawn toward violent programs. Given the choice, I know that my boys in particular will opt for cartoons with lots of fighting, edited at a rapid pace, which leave them punch-drunk. Commercially driven children's television would not be saturated with violent programs if they weren't popular. Why do children seem to like them so much? One interesting theory suggests that children choose active violent programs because they compensate for the passivity of TV viewing. They may be slumped on the couch, but children can enjoy the stimulation of activity while remaining totally safe. Some theorists have even suggested that violence on TV has a positive purpose for children—that it allows them to experience the normal emotions that we are usually taught to deny, like fear, greed, power hunger, and rage. After all, traditional children's stories have always been pretty gruesome, as "Red Riding Hood" and "Hansel and Gretel" can testify. These are thought-provoking ideas, but at the end of the day parents have to trust their instincts, and mine tell me that a surfeit of aggressive TV is not the best way to nurture a child's spirit.

PESTER POWER

"I want one of those" is a familiar refrain heard by parents when their children are watching the ads that are peppered throughout children's programs on commercial channels. Sweden is so concerned about the pressure put on parents to buy, buy, buy that it is now illegal there to advertise to children under the age of twelve. A study of Dutch children from the University of Amsterdam found that between 40 and 67 percent of children interviewed requested an item that had been advertised during the Saturday morning programs they watched in the weeks leading up to Christmas.

Another study, conducted at the University of Hertfordshire in the UK, has shown that the children who watch the most TV request the highest number of gifts in their letters to Santa Claus, and they are also more likely to ask for branded goods (a "Barbie," for example, rather than a doll). If you are worried that your child is too materialistic, then avoiding advertising may be a very good idea.

Those who are concerned about children's health are particularly worried about the foods that are advertised to our youngest generation. Recent research concluded that almost without exception foods featured were the so-called "big four": presugared breakfast cereals, soft drinks, candy, and savory snacks. There are also reports that food advertising to children does have a strong effect on their preferences, purchase behavior, and consumption. Consequently, high television use in children has become associated with the growing epidemic of childhood obesity in the West.

DELAYED DEVELOPMENT

The physical act of watching television may be harmful to young children. Some scientists believe that watching TV shuts down half of the brain—the left side, which is used for critical and analytical thinking. Screen images are made up of hundreds of dots, formed into lines. These put a strain on our vision, since the eye and brain are not designed to record visual stimuli at such a pace. We need to glue our eyes to the screen to make sense of what is going on, and in so doing mental activity is shut down. One experiment showed that within 30 seconds of TV viewing, brainwaves switched from beta waves (associated with alert attention) to alpha waves (associated with a relaxed, inattentive state). This may have far-reaching consequences for young children, argues Martin Large, author of *Set Free Childhood*.[1] "Healthy movement, repetition, play, conversation, and multisensory stimulation are all essential for healthy interconnections to be forged between the right and left sides of the brain. Static viewing fails to do this and actively inhibits development of the left side of the brain," he says. Large links excessive television viewing when very young with a long list of problems, including: attention deficit disorder, delayed speech, impaired hearing, shortsightedness, distorted spatial awareness, and balance, movement, and posture problems.

MEANINGFUL ALTERNATIVES

The issue here is not so much harmful programs, but what a child might otherwise be doing if he or she were not watching them. A bit like a handful of salty peanuts, television is easy to graze on, and the linkage between programs encourages us to stay glued. In a study of TV-free families conducted by Eastern Washington University, it was found that parents in these families had about an hour of meaningful conversation per day with their children, compared to a national average of just thirty-eight minutes per week. That's a massive difference. Another study, by the Harvard School of Public Health, found that children who don't have a television in their bedroom watch about forty minutes less television daily than those who do, and spend twenty minutes more reading or doing homework. And, of course, TV is not a real-life activity: it's passive and requires very little of children. Instead of watching football on TV and seeking prepackaged entertainment, they may be far better off playing football and engaging in imaginative play.

WHAT TO DO ABOUT TELEVISION

At the beginning of our TV-free Lent the children moaned pitifully about the loss of their favorite shows. However, surprisingly quickly they stopped asking and happily played with their toys instead. I probably missed their television viewing more than they did. My babysitter had gone. It was a particular loss early in the morning on Saturday, a time when John and I love to sleep in. I also habitually use the television to pacify the children so that I can free myself for an hour to cook the evening meal. Instead I played them story cassette tapes, which did help but sadly didn't freeze them spellbound in quite the same way that Walt Disney or Bob the Builder can. It was an interesting family experiment, during which John and I found ourselves reading and listening to the radio more, and catching up with rows that we should have had earlier. Come Good Friday, however, we were down at the electrics store buying a new TV set, and rejoicing at the prospect of the screen delights to come. We enjoy television, and it certainly eases some of the stresses that come with lively children and exhausted parents. What has changed is that I am now more determined to limit our television usage. On average the children clock up about four to five hours of TV during the week, and nearly the same again at weekends (but less in the summer). They watch videos more than television so that John and I have more control over what they are viewing. At this juncture I am content with this level of TV use, although others might see it as too much.

Lisa and Matt for instance have decided to go without television altogether, except for special occasions, like Christmas, when they borrow a TV. Lisa didn't like the way TV had affected her own home life. "My dad always had the TV on and it killed any conversation," she remembers. Their two children, Ezra, five, and Nellie, two, rarely complain about the lack of TV in their life.

"Ezra is able to entertain himself and go away and play very elaborate games by himself. We also have more time to talk to each other and pursue other interests," says Lisa. Music is a big part of family life, and Lisa often plays the piano or flute in the evening. "We also read together and play games. We are very lucky in that Matt works part time and we spend an enormous amount of time together as a family." Lisa says that Ezra is a very calm boy, articulate, with good concentration levels, and she does wonder whether it's because there has been so little TV in his life.

HOW TO TEACH YOUR CHILD
SPIRITUALLY HEALTHY TV HABITS

- ♣ Talk to your children about the negative effects of TV. Older children might want to read some of the facts presented in this chapter. What do they think they should do to have healthy TV habits?
- ♣ Resist buying a personal TV set for your child's bedroom.
- ♣ Set TV-viewing time limits—in Steiner schools it is recommended that children watch TV only on weekends. The American Academy of Pediatrics suggests restricting viewing to one or two hours per day, with no TV at all for children under two.
- ♣ Keep your mealtimes TV-free.
- ♣ Consider placing your television in a cabinet, to be brought out as and when you want it.
- ♣ Plan your children's television viewing with them in advance, and only turn the TV on for your chosen programs. Teach them how to be selective and choose programs that are likely to nourish their soul.
- ♣ Provide alternatives to TV, like a visit to the park, an after-school activity, or a family games evening.
- ♣ Use a VHS player to tape quality TV programs and fast forward the ads.
- ♣ Check the ratings on films and do not let your children watch films that are not suitable for their age.

➤ Set a good example by practicing good TV habits your-self. If you use the box as moving wallpaper your children are likely to do the same.

IT'S NOT ALL BAD

Television can be a great resource for your children if used selectively. It provides opportunities for them to learn about new things and places in the world. It can expand their range of interests and awareness of important global issues. Quality dramas and films are cheaply and conveniently available on video and DVD, some of which have themes that help children find meaning to life. And who said everything has to be worthy to be valuable? TV can also provide relaxation, laughter, and fun.

COMPUTER GAMES

Many computer and video games are educational, and thought to be good for hand-to-eye coordination and for promoting cognitive abilities and IT skills. Most psychologists and child development experts agree that limited play with these types of games is useful. However, there is concern about games that are violent, displaying graphic images of fighting, reckless driving, and death. The fact that the action is depicted in cartoon form does not necessarily make it any less disturbing. So called "shoot-'em up" games are particularly worrying, for they give the player the impression that he is the one doing the blasting. Evidence is contradictory as to whether playing these violent games leads to violent behavior in children, but they are known to be highly addictive and can cause sleep problems when used excessively. But do parents really need an academic study to provide them with a wisdom they already have? Prolonged play of this type is not healthy for a child's soul. It draws a child into a private fantasy world where violence is enjoyed and understood as a way of solving problems, and women are often depicted as sexual playthings. It does nothing that positively nurtures a child's inner life, and it commandeers time that might otherwise be spent in creative, sporting, or social pursuits. Parents need to supervise carefully children's computer play, ensuring that they use only games classified for their age. Choose games together and go for nonviolent ones, which can be fun and educational. Avoid having gaming platforms in children's bedrooms, and set time limits together for on-screen play.

SPIRITUAL PRACTICE FOR PARENTS

Examine your own TV habits. How much TV do you watch each week? What do you think about this level of viewing? How does it compare to the amount of TV you would ideally allow your children to watch? If you are concerned, experiment by having a TV-free week and explore new alternative activities. What do you find yourself doing?

23

Practice Animal Care

All things bright and beautiful, All creatures great and small, All things wise and wonderful, The Lord God made them all.

C. F. ALEXANDER

I HAVE AN EMPTY plastic tank by my desk as I write. I bought it today for my son, who is intent on keeping stick insects in his bedroom. The boy next door introduced him to this creepy crawly pastime, and will also provide the insects to start his terrarium. My son is very excited, and I imagine these extraordinary living twigs are going to be the focus of much attention amongst his visiting schoolfriends.

Children are usually very interested in animals. Most will ask for a pet at some stage; they love reading about all manner of creatures in books or watching them in films, and they adore visiting farms, zoos, and aquariums. The hamster or tadpole in the classroom is always a great source of delight, as are the goldfish in the doctor's surgery. This special relationship that children have with animals is not new. Archaeologists in the 1970s uncovered a Stone Age burial tomb in which was a small boy cradling a puppy, presumably his treasured companion. If your circumstances permit, the right animal in the home can teach your children many spiritual lessons, as well as be generally beneficial for their well-being.[1]

ANIMALS AND WELL-BEING

The health benefits of keeping a dog or cat are now well documented. Dogs have been used therapeutically in children's hospitals for some time, and research has shown that cats and dogs are a good stress reducer, lowering blood pressure. Children from pet-owning families are less likely to take time off school for sickness, says a study from the University of Warwick in the UK. The saliva of 138 children was tested, alongside inspection of their school attendance records. The saliva was tested for immunoglobulin A, which gives an indication of immune system function. It was shown that the pet owners benefited by up to eighteen extra half-days schooling each year and their immune systems were more stable. Early exposure to cats and dogs, before the age of one, may also reduce the likelihood of developing allergies.

Animals might also improve a child's behavior: a study of thirty-seven elementary schools in Australia found the presence of a cat increased classroom cohesiveness and atmosphere. The children were calmer and less disruptive when kitty was around.

THE LESSONS OF ANIMAL CARE

Children learn a tremendous amount from their pets, including responsibility and animal welfare. "Pet keeping can offer much in the way of educational opportunities," says June McNicholas, a psychologist at the University of Warwick who studies the relationships between pets and their owners. "What animals need to keep healthy or what happens if they are ill. Sometimes these can be useful analogies to the child's own experiences." That wet-nosed fluff ball can bring out the best in youngsters, and often really seems to touch their soul. "There's an instinct in very young children to care for and be mindful of small and helpless creatures," says Gail Melson, a professor of developmental studies at Purdue University, who has studied children and animals. She says that boys often withdraw from nurturing games at three or four, but not where their pets are concerned. For this reason she believes them to be a particularly valuable experience for boys.

Pets can teach some profound life lessons. The pregnancy of a cat, mouse, or dog and the subsequent birth of a litter are utterly thrilling for a child, and may leave a deep imprint about what is miraculous. More painfully, a pet is likely to provide children with their first experience of death. I can remember, aged nine, the distress of cradling my cold, stiff, dead hamster in my palm, tenderly wrapping her in tissue paper and burying her beneath a tree. I used to put flowers on her grave, which my father had thoughtfully marked with an engraved plaque. In subsequent years there came the death of fish, a cat, and a dog. Tears were shed for all, but with each mourning, the confusing abstract notion of death got a little bit more understandable.

When we connect with animals we break through the artificial barriers that separate us from the natural world. Children may remember that they are part of a greater world, one that lies beyond their home, school, and street. They may remember that a single sacred life force pulses through us all, and that we all share the same needs for food and water, light and warmth, shelter, freedom to move, freedom to be.

Children easily empathize with animal suffering. They are often enthusiastic supporters of animal welfare organizations, and are dedicated rescuers of stray baby birds and injured squirrels. Becoming aware of the suffering of others is a vital part of a spiritual journey, and animals seem to have the power to stir up compassion in the young and therefore can play an important part in their development. Conversely, sometimes children can be cruel to animals. They may pinch and maul them, and sometimes kill insects. There is, I think, an element of sadism in children, which, combined with a thrill for power, can manifest in animal cruelty. Keep an eye out for this type of behavior, show your disapproval, and encourage respect and kindness.

Companion pets are of special value in the home because they provide children with unconditional love. When there are struggles in children's lives, dogs or cats can be a great source of comfort and strength. They are very good at simply being there, as a witness to human unhappiness. Cats are tremendous centers of calm, while dogs seem to be empathetic. Their naturally exuberant nature serves to remind children of the delight there is to be had in life. An animal's nonjudgmental affection keeps a child's heart space open, and maintains a link to a world in which there is goodness.

PET PITFALLS

Pets can have a novelty value for children, and they may fail to care for them properly once they tire of their new friend. Parents often find that they have to take over the regular chores of cleaning and feeding. There are important life lessons to be learned here about commitment and responsibility, and children need to be urged to keep up everyday care. As in all relationships, real love is found not only during the honeymoon period, but also in the routine work of the day-to-day.

Before you take on a pet, give good consideration to your family's ability to care for it. Does your child have the commitment, and the ability, to look after an animal properly? If not, do you have the time to do it?

If your lifestyle doesn't suit a pet, there are other ways you can provide your children with an animal experience—feeding wild birds, adopting a zoo animal, or helping out at a farm. And with one of the kits now available you can watch a chrysalis turn into a butterfly, or keep worms for a while in a glass tank. Offering to look after a friend's pet while he or she goes on vacation is another way to add an extra valuable member to the family occasionally.

SPIRITUAL PRACTICE FOR PARENTS

ANIMAL MEDITATION

If you already have a pet in the family, this is an opportunity to look at it more carefully. Alternatively, you could focus your attention on a wild animal.

Look at your chosen animal. Really look at it. Notice its size and color, the way it moves. See the texture of its fur, feathers, or scales. See the color and form of its eyes. What is its personality? How does this animal make you feel?

Look more deeply at this animal. Consider its wondrous biological design. You could not make this animal, no matter what materials you had at your disposal. Think about the elaborate network that gave life to this animal and sustains it: air, water, soil, sun, plants, other life forms. Think about the evolution of this animal: the distant ancestors that have been perfecting themselves over thousands of years to give birth to the creature now before you. Marvel at this animal.

Honor Silence
in the Home

Nothing is so like God as silence.

MEISTER ECKHART

FAMILIES ARE NATURALLY very noisy. Babies and toddlers are likely to erupt at any time of the day or night, and the play of children at all ages is rippled with laughter, chatter, and shouting. The racket of computer games, music, television, and battery-operated toys can all add to the hubbub.

One particular part of my day has all the volume and mayhem of a flock of geese gathering to migrate: the morning school run. On bad days it is a time of last-minute tears, protests about what's been packed in the lunch box, and instructions being hollered about missing shoes and book bags. The quiet moment after the children have all been safely dispatched, envelopes me like a wonderfully soft duvet.

When my three children were all preschoolers, they used to shout and scream a great deal. At the time we were living in a basement apartment, and I was very worried about disturbing the elderly woman who lived above us. She was a practicing Buddhist and seemed to relish a quiet and orderly lifestyle. Hers was the sort of home where wind chimes tinkled and cats sat on the windowsill yawning. One day, when I met her outside, I apologized for the cacophony happening beneath her and asked her to let me know if things got too much to bear. I was much impressed by her wisdom when she shrugged her shoulders nonchalantly and said, "Noise, children don't make noise, they make sounds. That is very different to noise. Noise is a horrible thing, when someone plays their music too loud or drills the wall late at night. The shouts and cries of a child is new life finding its way in the world. I don't get disturbed by that." I was so relieved, and later tried to remember her thoughtful words when I myself felt overwhelmed by family sounds. I remember too the words of a Catholic priest at a christening I attended. During a solemn moment of quiet prayer a baby started bawling. The priest threw up his arms in pleasure and proclaimed, "Thank God there's new life in this church!"

Silence is a necessary ingredient for a spiritual life. I have periodically gone on short retreats to a Benedictine monastery, and there you find the sort of sumptuous silence that you can melt into. This is a sacred silence, where you get the chance not only to hear yourself think, but also to stop those head conversations, and instead hum along to a tune that comes from a deeper place, your inner core. "Let us be silent that we may hear the whispers of the gods," wrote Ralph Waldo Emerson.

These moments of sacred silence become incredibly rare when you have children. The absence of stillness and silence is probably one of the things I have found hardest about parenthood. You simply don't get much silence, and children can be so demanding that your need for it may be greater than it has ever been in your life before. So what's the solution? How can we bring something of the monastery into a home full of sounds?

SPECIAL QUIET TIME

In the monastery I visit, every night after evening prayer the monks and nuns maintain complete silence. This is the time to let go of all the work and talk of the day and journey inward. "There are times when good words are to be left unsaid out of esteem for silence," said St. Benedict. It would be unrealistic and oppressive to try to impose this rule on a family home, but you can achieve something of its flavor. When you have gone through the usual nighttime routines and put your children to bed, teach them to observe this time that veils their day from night as their special "quiet" time. It may only be a moment if they are tired, or it may be half an hour or so if they are not ready to sleep. Turn the music and television off, ask them to stop chattering, and encourage reading or quiet activity. Don't impose this in a punitive way, but make it into a cozy treat that they will enjoy. As a family, value silence. Quiet time is something that children grow into, and if you would like them to learn how to pray or meditate it's a good preparation.

PARENTS' QUIET TIME

You need regular special quiet time too—evenings when there are no distractions from the television, phone calls, visitors, or administrative tasks. When the chores are done, give yourself the space to sit and restore yourself in God's healing silence. If you are an early bird, like my husband, you may find that the morning provides you with an opportunity for silence. John frequently gets up at five AM, while the family are still asleep, to practice a short meditation and have some quiet to himself.

We live in a society that values constant activity, and in the twenty-four-hour whirl that marks much of urban life it can be hard to find a pocket of stillness in which to smell the roses. In the words of the Sufi poet Rumi: "Only let the moving waters calm down, and the sun and moon will be reflected on the surface of your being." Do something mindful that nourishes your soul, whether it's simply sitting, reading an inspiring book, or keeping a journal. Evenings when your children are in bed may be the only opportunity you get to have a chunk of time during which you can hear the voice deep inside that gives direction to your life. Make the most of it.

SPIRITUAL PRACTICE FOR PARENTS

Sneak a minute of silence into your life as part of your daily routine. If you look for it, sixty seconds of quiet can be found in the most unlikely places. You might find it at your desk before you start work. Or it could be while waiting for a saucepan to boil, or in the car after you have dropped all the kids off at school. There's a moment of silence to be found after watching the evening news, and another moment hidden in the yard after having hung up the laundry. Where can you find one?

GOING OUT
INTO THE WORLD

Use Nature as a Spiritual Teacher

The best remedy for those who are afraid, lonely, or unhappy is to go outside, somewhere where they can be quiet, alone with the heavens, nature, and God. Because only then does one feel that all is as it should be and that God wishes to see people happy, amidst the simple beauty of nature.

The Diary of Anne Frank

WHEN WE BAPTIZED our first son, Benedict, as part of the ceremony we filed outside the church and the priest held him aloft under a giant magnolia tree, which was in magnificent full bloom at the time. I read a prayer that I had written for Benedict, in which I honored his place in nature. It was an acknowledgment that we were welcoming our son not just into a community of people, but also into the created world. We wanted to give thanks to the earth and the ancient stars from which he came. It's an awesome thought that our precious infant, who the priest held high in her hands that day, began his life fifteen billion years ago, when the universe flashed into being.

The Native Americans have a beautiful image that newborns emerge into the world through the sipapuni, or earth navel. Some scientists now have a similar understanding of how we come to life through the evolution of natural forces. Hydrogen, said one astronomer, is a light odorless gas that, given enough time, turns into people.

Since we are made of the stuff of the universe, it seems self-evident that communing with nature will provide us with a deeper experience of ourselves. Jesus often used earth stories and parables to help us understand life in its fullness, and he encouraged his followers to learn basic spiritual messages from seeds and vines. When we experience the greatness of a mountain, the expansiveness of the sea, we understand that we are part of something larger than "I," a mere mortal, contained within an envelope of skin.

Some evolutionary psychologists believe we are genetically programmed with an affinity for the outdoors. They call it "biophilia," and numerous studies have shown that natural outdoor environments are good for our physical and psychological well-being. We know instinctively that if we are in need of restoration we should take ourselves away on a vacation to the sea or countryside. At weekends after a frazzled week in an urban setting, we turn to gardening and walking the dog. "An individual's harmony with his or her 'own deep self' requires not merely a journey to the interior but a harmonizing with the environmental world," writes James Hillman, a leading Jungian analyst, who is one of the pioneers of "ecopsychology."[1] This is the term used to describe an emerging synthesis of psychology and ecology. According to ecopsychologists, mainstream psychology has limited its understanding of mental health to what's going on within the psyche of the individual and his or her family relationships. It is a process of looking inward, but ecopsychology teaches us to look outward too, and attend to how we relate to nature. "Ecopsychology proceeds from the assumption that at its deepest level the psyche remains sympathetically bonded to the Earth that mothered us into existence," writes Theodore Roszak, author of a seminal book in the field, *The Voice of the Earth*. [2] Crucially, a deep relationship with nature will not only help us be more fulfilled, happy human beings, but also make us look anew at how we treat the planet, which we are currently polluting and destroying as if it were a dead and servile place.

We all need to feel the sun on our face, the wind on our back, and the grass between our toes. Children are no exception. Even very young babies take great sensuous delight when they experience warm water or a breeze on their skin, or see dappled sunlight through a canopy of trees.

Children are instinctively drawn toward fantasy forests, animal characters, and fairy stories set in nature. Their love of pets and visits to a zoo or farm are all testament to the strong connections they feel to the natural world. Camping out in the great outdoors is one of the greatest adventures of childhood. Ask any Girl or Boy Scout.

Today's children, especially those in urban settings, don't get too many opportunities to be outside in nature. Time outdoors is being squeezed out of their lives. Some schools have reduced playtime to maximize on teaching time and avoid bad playground behavior. Field trips are in decline because teachers find that the complex health and safety regulations, and the threat of litigation if there were to be an accident, simply make the outing too much trouble. And parents, fearful of abductions and traffic, wrap their loved ones up in a hermetically sealed electronic world. Additionally, according to Alan Dyer, Coordinator of Environmental Education at Plymouth University in the UK, both parents and teachers are themselves anxious about their lack of countryside knowledge: "They say, 'I don't know a daisy from a dandelion, how can I take children out?' They are very fearful of their own ignorance."

Children enjoy being outside in a different way to adults. While grown-ups are usually passive, appreciating the scenery, children are busy finding out what nature can do. They do all the messy things that would be frowned on indoors, such as making mud pies and camps. They interact with nature, digging trenches and filling them with water, climbing trees and collecting snails. Long and complex games can be played with the simplest things—a puddle, a stick, a hideaway in a tree. They are interested in the detail of nature, things they can get right up close to and touch. "Children can't handle big landscapes," says Alan Dyer. "It's simply too big for them and outside of their experience. I have seen an amusing cartoon of a mom and dad looking out across the Grand Canyon with awesome appreciation, while beside them their son plays with a Gameboy."

As a spiritual parent you can provide your children with as much opportunity as possible to enjoy the natural world and encourage their sense of wonder and delight in it. In our family at present this translates into something very simple: at weekends we leave the city as often as possible and go out on walks together. We go pond dipping, bug hunting, blackberry picking, and tree climbing. We collect leaves, fir cones, fallen birds' nests and shells, and bring them home for display or artwork. We grow hyacinth bulbs and sunflower seeds. During the week we go to the park and beach whenever we can.

There are countless ways in which you and your family can experience nature together—and you don't have to leave the city.[3] An urban nature reserve provides a delightful oasis, and many run educational programs for children. And if you have a yard or garden, all manner of miracles can be cultivated there.

HOW TO SHARE NATURE WITH YOUR CHILD

Joseph Cornell, an international leading expert in children's nature education from the United States, has written a number of best-selling books on the subject, most notably *Sharing Nature With Children*.[4] He offers some helpful advice as to how you can help your child grow spiritually through nature.

- Share your feelings about what you see, hear, feel, taste, and touch.
- Share your feelings of awe and respect.
- Be in the moment by really being aware yourself, and listening to your child.
- Focus the child's attention and set the tone for the experience.
- Save any explanations about what you are witnessing until after the child has had the opportunity to experience it directly.
- Talk about what was seen after it has been experienced.
- Don't worry about needing to know the exact names of tree, plant, or animal species.
- Allow a sense of joy and delight to permeate the experience.

Alan Dyer says that after a child's awareness about something in nature has been raised, the next step is for her to find a way of expressing her sense of awe. He recommends artwork, painting, or drawing, or making simple sculptures.

If your child seems uninterested and detached, don't pressure her or feel that you are failing. You cannot force a child to catch a glimpse of the transcendent, no matter how loudly that river is singing to you, or the flowers are laughing, or trees applauding. Be happy in that you are providing the opportunity for your child to experience nature, then step back and trust that it will eventually work its own magic in her heart.

NATURE GAMES

Alan Dyer suggests the following games that parents can play with their children for raising awareness of nature and for fun.

The Listening Game

Sit quietly with your child somewhere in nature and ask him to close his eyes. Now encourage him to listen very carefully to all the sounds around him: the rustle of leaves, birdsong, maybe the hum of distant traffic. When he has finished get him to make a sound map. This is a large sheet of paper with a cross in the middle representing where he sits. Ask him to draw images that in some way express the sounds he has heard, mapping their positions in relation to the cross on the paper.

Collecting colors

Ask your child to collect as many colors in nature as she can find. These can include the varied green hues of leaves (or russet if in autumn), bright petals, and berries, and the browns of tree bark and earth. The exercise can also teach your child about nature stewardship—that it's OK to pick a petal, but not to pull up a whole plant—and about the perils of berries and fungi, which shouldn't be eaten without adult supervision. Your child may want to take her colorful collection home and make a collage with them.

A Cocktail of Smells

Invite your child to collect in a plastic cup as many different smells as he can find in nature. Flowers, leaves, pine cones, and earth all have strong odors, some of which your child will find pleasant and others he may not. Get him to explore the different smells and comment on his preferences.

A night-time walk

This is a truly thrilling experience for a child. Take your child out on a flashlight-lit walk in the dark woods or park. Take another family with you if you feel there is more safety in numbers. Candles carried in jam jars on strings make a charming alternative to flashlights. The intention of this is not to scare your child with spooky stories, but to encourage her to feel comfortable in the woods, and to befriend the darkness. A full moon and cloudless sky make the experience all the more amazing.

STARGAZING

Nothing produces a sense of awe and wonder on quite such a scale as the stars at night. Staring out into the sparkling garden of the universe we feel ourselves to be transported to a vast and timeless realm. Many children still sing the nursery rhyme "Twinkle, twinkle little star, / How I wonder what you are!," but not so many are given the chance to go out at night and lose themselves in contemplation of the heavens above.

Light pollution in cities makes it difficult to see stars clearly, and the busyness of our lives often means that we do not take the time to practice the oldest science, astronomy. Take your children stargazing. Plan it as a special party evening, with invited friends and family, a nighttime picnic and a sense of occasion, and the children will find it a thrilling adventure. For best results you will need a clear night, preferably far away from artificial light. You will see about ten times as many stars if you get out of town into the countryside. Take flashlights, but cover them with red tissue paper or fabric to mask their brightness: it takes the eyes about thirty minutes to adjust to the dark. If you have binoculars or a telescope all the better, and for added educational value you could take with you maps of the stars for reference. Star atlases are available in bookshops, so too are planispheres: these are star maps on a disk that can be adjusted. Star maps are also available to download online.[5]

Play dot-to-dot with the stars, making up patterns and images out of the constellations. This age-old pastime has led to great mythological stories from all cultures about the celestial beings found in the night sky.[6] You could tell the children one of these mythological stories, or make up one of your own. These wondrous old tales will give your children a sense of how humankind has struggled to understand the mystery of the universe, as well as infuse your star party with extra sparkle.

TEACH YOUR CHILDREN TO BE FRIENDS OF THE EARTH

It's increasingly easy to recycle in the home, making sure that our waste paper, bottles, jars, tins, textiles, and more, are put back into the system to reduce our plunder of natural resources. Children are frequently very devoted to recycling, and readily seem to understand and feel committed to principles of waste reduction. Get them involved in your recycling at home so that they are brought up with a keen awareness of its ecological benefits. You can also encourage children to reuse disposable items like paper bags and scrap paper, and to use refillable lunch containers. Children can see from our example how to reduce waste—by not buying products with excess packaging, switching off lights at home, and walking rather than using the car for short journeys. Get them involved too in making green consumer choices when shopping.

A SPIRITUAL PRACTICE FOR PARENTS

Take yourself out into nature and enjoy this "beauty walk," as recommended by John R. Stowe in *The Findhorn Book of Connecting with Nature*.[7] He writes: "As you set out, ask yourself to focus on 'beauty.' Ask your eyes, ears, all your senses, to show you the beauty in this place; then just walk. As you do, repeat this request over and over in your mind: 'Show me the beauty. Show me the beauty.' Then, see what you notice."

26

Seek Out
Kindred Spirits

Thee lift me up and I'll lift thee, and we will ascend together.

Quaker proverb

WHEN I FIRST moved to Brighton from London, with three
preschool children, I felt desperately lonely. I can remember the empty feeling that settled upon me as my husband left at
six in the morning, bound for a ten-hour stint in the capital, and
an agonizingly long day stretched ahead of me, with no adult
company other than a voice on the radio or telephone. Most of us
do not thrive well without companionship, and parenting, particularly for stay-at-home mothers, can be a very isolating experience. Moving away from family and friends, as many of us do,
compounds the feeling of disconnection. Being a lone parent
makes us even more vulnerable to isolation.

People in the past would not have faced such problems. We
would have lived in stable homogenous groups, with extended
family nearby. We would have known all our neighbors.
Geographic and social mobility has widened the life options open
to us and brought diversity, but often the price we pay is loneliness.
Social bonds are the most powerful predictor of life satisfaction. The
more we are plugged into a social network, the happier we are.

That's the view of social scientist Professor Robert Putnam, who has recently published a surprising best seller, *Bowling Alone*,[1] which argues that people in the United States are becoming increasingly isolated from their neighbors, friends, and families, and that loneliness is as common a cause of illness as cigarette smoking. Professor Putnam's book is based on a huge sweep of survey and data analysis, plus 500,000 interviews over the last twenty-five years. He demonstrates that North American families have dinner together only two-thirds as often as they did one generation ago, and that they spend 35 percent less time visiting friends than thirty years ago. They are less likely to belong to organizations that meet regularly, and more likely to bowl alone than belong to a league.

What has all this to do with family spirituality? Few of us can develop our spirituality by walking the path of the hermit. From the most ancient times we have banded together into fellowship groups, finding that being in spiritual community magnifies our individual efforts. We need to be with people who share a common spiritual vision and can offer each other support and encouragement. The spiritual community is a place where we share our wisdom and help each other maintain a spiritual practice. Men and women have lived in monasteries, gathered in congregations, sanghas, prayer or house groups, covens or sweat lodges. In a world that is becoming socially threadbare, these soul connections are becoming harder to find. It is especially difficult for parents to seek them out, given that we live in a society that is not noted for being child-friendly. Many spiritual/religious groups and organizations are not geared to cater for children, and trying to join in as a family is an impossibility. I have fled from a church crying because being present with a lively toddler provoked hostility from the congregation. When it comes to the new forms of spirituality that are emerging, mind, body, and spirit activities that include children are few and far between.

CHILDREN NEED SPIRITUAL COMMUNITY, TOO

It isn't only grown-ups who benefit from spiritual companionship. One of the things that we find in our church is that children are eager to go to Sunday School because of the friendships they have with each other. Mine get very excited about the possibility of who they might be able to spend time with. Parents often nurture those friendships by arranging play dates. As children grow up they are eager to fit in, and not be seen to be different from their friends. It's very reassuring and supportive for them to have a peer group that shares the family's spiritual beliefs and practices.

I think it's essential too for them to be around adults who are positive spiritual role models, and to witness grown-ups participating in meaningful worship. These experiences can imprint on children very deeply, possibly in an unconscious way, like a hidden reservoir of realness that may provide a spiritual wellspring in future times of drought.

FINDING SPIRITUAL COMMUNITY

"The only way to have a friend is to be one," said Ralph Waldo Emerson. Families have to be proactive in the creation of communities that are spiritually sustaining. If you want family fellowship you may have to be prepared to work hard to create it, especially if you are outside of any formal religious structures. Choose to be optimistic: there are other people who are hungry for soul connection too. Here are some ideas.

Start a conversation

If you care about your spirituality, talk about it to others. In her book *Turning to One Another*,[2] organization consultant Margaret Wheatley argues: "Large and successful change efforts start with conversations among friends, not with those in power. 'Some friends and I started talking . . .' Change doesn't happen from a leader announcing the plan. Change begins from deep inside the system, when a few people notice something they will no longer tolerate, or respond to a dream of what's possible."

Resist the urge to stay silent and apart, and instead initiate a conversation about your spiritual beliefs. This isn't about ringing people's doorbells and evangelizing your take on life's great mysteries. This is about a sensitively timed mutual sharing. You will soon pick up whether there is common ground, and from these first simple conversations informal spiritual networks and friendships can grow.

Consider joining an organized religion

Undoubtedly the easiest way to find spiritual fellowship is by joining the existing structures. If you don't already belong to one of the major faiths, look again at what is on offer. If there is enough of a match between where you are at spiritually and the practice and doctrines of a faith, it may be worth exploring further. My husband John and I have in the past done some serious church shopping, trying to find a community that might share our liberal Christian faith. We worshipped with Unitarians for a while, and are currently with an Anglican church. In both cases we have needed to invest energy in revitalizing the children's ministry that was on offer. If we want to have a flourishing spiritual space for our children, I think we have to be prepared to roll up our sleeves and help make it happen. Similarly, a group of Buddhist mothers I know are looking at ways in which they can develop their children's group.

Host spiritual activities for like-minded friends and family members

There are many ideas in this book for family rituals, creative pursuits, and activities in nature. Are there any other families who would like to join you? Invite others around for a storytelling evening, or plan to go out stargazing together. Host an Easter egg hunt in your garden or local park or go on a Halloween owl prowl. The children will find these events especially thrilling if there are other children coming along.

Look out for meaningful family events

Keep your eyes open for organized events that are in harmony with the spiritual practice you want to develop in the family.

These may not be expressly spiritual, but nevertheless are in step with your spiritual journeying. Conservation groups such as The Sierra Club and the National Wildlife Federation increasingly offer nature-based activities for families (see note 3 for Chapter 25).

Some of the summer festivals can also be very family friendly, offering lots of creative activities for parents and children.

Form your own spiritual parenting group

If you can start enough conversations with enough people, there may be sufficient numbers to start a fellowship circle. There are many models for small groups, but I am drawn to the "wisdom circle" tradition. This is a discussion group based on those used by councils of indigenous peoples, and the circle-forming traditions such as Quaker meetings. The purpose is to speak and listen from the heart, to share, heal, and grow. Meetings start with a simple ritual of the group's choosing (lighting a candle and placing a photograph of your children in the center of the circle may work well). Have a mutually agreed subject for discussion for the occasion, and use a talking stick passed from one to another to structure the sharing. Resist the temptation to cross-talk or give advice, unless it is requested. And, importantly, value the silence that there might be between the words. If you are interested in setting up a group of this type there are various helpful guidebooks available.[3]

Explore the Internet

Corresponding in cyberspace is not as satisfying as real face-to-face contact, but it can still be a very positive experience. If you are tied to the home, it may be one of the only ways you can reach out to others. It is my hope that through this book like-minded parents may be able to contact each other through my Web site: parentingwithspirit.co.uk. If I can put you in contact with each other, I will. And there will probably be other chat rooms, e-mail newsletters, and Web sites that hit the mark for you. I've listed some at the end of this book that I have found useful. Happy surfing.

Remember that everyone is a potential kindred spirit

We can be picky and choosy about people, selecting only those we find attractive, or who we think will provide something for us. We have become very adept at making quick, and often brutal, judgments about people and their worth. There is a strong tendency for us to seek out only people who we think are the same as ourselves. Of course, we need people in our lives with whom we feel there is a big overlap, but what about all the others? Daily we come across people who are different to ourselves, and who we may dismiss as not worth our while. But if we took the time to know these people's stories a little better, we might realize that there is more commonality between us than we first supposed. Those harsh assessments that we first make about each other may be softened if we find out something of each other's history and how we have got to be where we are right now. If we can be curious enough, and brave enough, to share a little of ourselves with each other, despite our differences, we might find that our social network becomes rich beyond belief.

SPIRITUAL PRACTICE FOR PARENTS

Take a moment to close your eyes and allow yourself to dream a little . . .

Imagine you are with your family on a long journey up a hill. At the top you meet a group of welcoming people who invite you to join them in their beautiful, sacred celebrations. Who are those people and what are they doing? How does this spiritual activity affect your family?

As you go back down the hill consider the ways in which you might be able to realize your vision in life here on earth. Who might you need to start a conversation with?

Inspire Kindness in Your Children

If you light a lamp for somebody, it will also brighten your path.

Buddhist saying

EACH CHRISTMAS MY children's school invites its students to fill a shoebox with toys, toiletries, and stationery to be taken to children in need in eastern Europe. It is a task they undertake with great pleasure, and I am often surprised by their generosity as they proffer some of their most cherished toys for consideration. They are horrified to think that somewhere, in places they have never been, there are children who do not have toys to play with or pens and paper to draw on. It is a gift they can understand far more than a donation of money. I can see Saint Francis's words—"It is in giving that we receive"—in action when I witness their glowing faces as they imagine that on Christmas morning a toyless child might be opening their box of treasures. A shoebox of toys is a miniscule gesture, I know, given the colossal inequalities in the world, yet, hopefully, it is of benefit, and it certainly offers a great teaching to my children: they learn that it feels good to give.

Every spiritual tradition has taught that acts of kindness are an essential part of our lives here on earth. Such an act is not a tiresome duty or obligation but, at its purest, an act of empathy, generosity, and love. When we give benevolently to others and to the living planet, we feel ourselves growing as human beings.

Kindness is an awareness we develop over time; it is a wisdom we learn experientially. Crucially, children need first to be the recipients of kindness, and if their parenting has been positive, there will have been much of this in evidence, for infants provide ample opportunity for us to dip into our wellspring of nurturing love. Kindness will naturally flow from an interest and concern for others, and this will come if there are loving and close relationships in your children's lives.

There then comes a time when you notice that your toddler is able to tap into his own human spirit and brighten someone else's path too. He probably still stamps his feet and yells "Mine!" a great deal, but there might also be a moment when he spontaneously shares a packet of candy with friends, gives someone a hug, draws you a picture, or helps carry plates to the table; these small acts all show that the spiritual practice of kindness is being discovered and its power harnessed. Children learn that the giving and receiving of kindness connects us to each other and produces a feeling of bliss. In the words of the Dalai Lama: "When we feel love and kindness toward others, it not only makes others feel loved and cared for, but it helps us also to develop inner happiness and peace."

PRACTICAL WAYS TO TEACH KINDNESS TO CHILDREN

We must look out for opportunities to encourage and support a child's learning about the spiritual practice of kindness. First and foremost, our children will watch and learn from us. Are we practicing kindness in our own lives? Do our children see us doing good turns for friends and neighbors? Do they hear us speaking graciously and listening intently to others? Do they witness us sharing our time, talents, and possessions with a generous heart? Do they observe us being compassionately concerned and involved in the wider world? There will be no greater lesson we can offer our children than that taught by our example. This then needs to be reinforced by encouragement and the creation of opportunities for children to experience the power of kindness for themselves. There are countless ways in which daily life presents such occasions. Here are few ideas.

- *When your children do something kind, give them praise.* Let them know that you have noticed what they have done, no matter how small, and that it was good and that it makes the world a better place.
- *Teach your children the importance of sharing.* From a young age you can encourage them to share their toys, food, and treats with playmates.
- *Get your children involved in the giving of gifts.* From a young age let them experience the pleasure of making and giving greeting cards and small presents.
- *Send greetings.* Encourage your children to make cards or small gifts for someone who is ill or having a difficult time.
- *Give them jobs to do around the home.* Lavish huge amounts of praise on your children when they help with chores, and watch them come back willing to do more.
- *Encourage your children to befriend a student at school who may be lonely.* If you know there is someone new starting in class, suggest that your child invite him or her to play.
- *Consider buying a pet.* The care of an animal presents children with many opportunities to practice nurturing care.
- *Look out for books in which the characters do something kind for each other.* Use the opportunity to discuss the story with your children.
- *Love your enemies.* Stress that it's essential to remain courteous even to those people we don't like right now. Teach children that forgiveness is a virtue that we need to work toward: we all make mistakes sometimes, and deserve another chance.
- *Make food to share.* When baking cakes or cookies with your children, make a few extra for them to give to someone.
- *Suggest your children write letters or make phone calls to say thank you.* If they have been on the receiving end of a kindness, help your children express their gratitude with a proper thank you.

❥ *Hold a "Secret Angel" day.* Put the names of the family members in a hat, and each take one. This is the person for whom you will secretly perform random acts of kindness. Surreptitiously do something nice for each other, whether it's slipping a special treat into a lunch box, making a bed, tidying a pile of CDs or leaving a compliment on a note under a pillow. At the end, discuss how it went, how it felt, and then have each secret angel reveal his or her identity.

❥ *Have a good deed day.* Decide that as a family you will do something kind today. Get the children to come up with ideas. Weeding grandma's garden, perhaps? Picking up garbage from the park? Taking someone's dog for a walk? The possibilities are many.

❥ *Practice the Buddhist meditation for loving kindness with your children (see Chapter 7).* This is a powerful way to "tenderize" our souls and nurture compassion.

❥ *Contemplate acts of kindness during bedtime prayer.* When assimilating the day during prayer, encourage your children to consider how kindness might have played a part. Do they feel grateful for any kindnesses they have received? Have they behaved kindly to someone? Do they regret not having been kind? You may want to make petitionary prayers for those in need.

KINDNESS IN THE COMMUNITY AND WIDER WORLD

Charitable giving and volunteering are part of the answer to many of our world's problems. Generate an attitude of service in your home, happily giving what you can to the local community and the world beyond your horizons. Parents can encourage and support children in this by giving them hands-on service opportunities that will help them understand their connection to society and the environment. If volunteer work and charitable giving starts at a young age, it may become something that children grow up to value as a worthwhile and enjoyable part of their lives.

You may be thinking that you simply don't have the time or energy to give any more to anyone else. Remember, people who do voluntary and charity work often say that they get back a lot more than they give, and what you do needn't take lots of time. Moreover, it can prove to be a fun and meaningful way to spend a few hours together as a family.

Initially children may be able to "piggyback" on you and any voluntary work that you do. Get them involved in simple tasks that help you out, and take them along to appropriate functions and events. From about fourteen, youngsters can become volunteers in their own right, and there are a number of organizations now that can support and guide them.

As soon as children are old enough to get pocket money they are old enough to give to charity. Even giving a few pennies a week teaches a child that giving and sharing are a central part of our life. There may be special causes that the whole family feels strongly about, or your children may develop their own burning issues. Many charities have junior branches that publish educational material alongside suggestions for young fund-raisers and activists. Schemes like "adopt an animal" or "sponsor a child" work well with children, because they provide a direct experience of how their gifts are of benefit. Schools also host fund-raising charitable events to which pocket money can be donated. Encourage your children not to look for anything in return, just to give freely, let it go, and take in the good feeling that comes with giving generously.

TEACHING MANNERS

Good manners, like saying "please" and "thank you," are not simply social niceties, they are in themselves acts of kindness. When said authentically, a courtesy makes someone feel valued and respected, and helps protect the speaker from feelings of superiority. There is a fair amount of rote learning with young children; daily I have to remind mine to say "please" when they ask for things, and we still have a long way to go with table manners. Getting young children to wait their turn to speak, instead of interrupting someone, is another huge challenge.

We often forget that the best way for children to learn good manners is for us to speak respectfully to them and to others. We should say "please" and "thank you" to our children, and say "sorry" when we know we have done them a wrong. We also have to display good table manners ourselves. My youngest son, when aged three, earnestly told off an adult guest for talking with her mouth full. At the time she was telling her young son, also three, to put his hand over his mouth when he coughed. We were all highly amused by the admonition, but he was right.

It is important that children treat their elders, including other parents and teachers, politely. We can teach children the common courtesies of social etiquette, like smiling and saying hello or good-bye, by our own example as well as direct coaching. We must also remember to speak respectfully about other people when the children are within earshot. If you describe the class teacher as a "complete idiot," you will only undermine your child's respect for him or her.

Notice when your children have been polite and respectful, and remember to say how pleased you are with them. A few words of timely heartfelt praise are worth a hundred reprimands.

Encourage Children's Big Questions

The answer my friend is blowing in the wind,
The answer is blowing in the wind.

BOB DYLAN

WITH MY ELDEST son it started at about age five, and two years later it's still going strong. It can happen at any moment, often completely out of the blue, during mundane moments: when squeezing toothpaste onto your child's brush or walking to school, while wiping a bottom. My friend's child woke up one morning, sat bolt upright in bed, bleary eyed, and began his day with one. Another mother told me that her seven-year-old son leaves them around the house for her in note form. We are talking about those huge ponderous questions that all children seem to ask spontaneously. Some of my favorites have included "Who made God?", "Does God get married?", "Is there Coca Cola in heaven?" and, more sadly, "Why do people kill each other?" and "When will I die?"

When young we have a basic yet profound curiosity about the world, born out of our sense of wonder and awe for the remarkable place in which we find ourselves existing. If Socrates was right when he said that "Philosophy begins in wonder," then children are off to a flying start.

"Children begin their lives with an amazing natural curiosity," says Robert Fisher, a professor of education and director of the Center for Research in Teaching Thinking at Brunel University in the UK "Among the many questions they ask will be open-ended philosophical questions, such as the five-year-old who asked me 'Where does time go when it is over?'"

While we can still count our age in single digits, even things that are commonplace are worthy of those brow-furrowing "why?" questions: "Why is the sky blue?", "Why does it get dark at night?", "Why is water wet" or "Why is fire hot?" David Hay, a researcher into children's spirituality, explains that a child's sense of mystery can be awakened by much more down-to-earth and familiar phenomena—simple events such as a flame appearing when a match is struck, or a light being switched on, or water coming out of a tap. "I myself remember my feeling of utter amazement and awe when it was demonstrated to me in the classroom that air has weight; before that time I had somehow got the idea that air was simply 'nothing,'" he says.

A distinction between the mundane, the silly, and the profound is not made by young children. In one breath a child might ask "What happens when you die?" and in the next breath ask "What's for tea?" or "What color was my poo when I was a baby?" Sometimes they ask the question without seeming to want an answer, as if they sense that much of life is incomprehensible, and that whatever explanation you give is likely to be inadequate. Their question is simply a sharing about something they are themselves contemplating. Pat Hannam, mother of three and a committee member of the educational charity The Society for the Advancement of Philosophical Enquiry and Reflection in Education, remembers that her children had lots of questions following the death of their grandmother. More recently her son asked, "When you die, do you want to?" Pat says she couldn't get further into that thought, "despite trying some open lines. I concluded it was the end of a process of thoughts that he was sharing rather than a question."

Pat advises that parents can encourage their children to engage in philosophical inquiry by asking open-ended questions. "When they come home from school these days I ask them whether they have had any interesting thoughts or asked any interesting questions," she says. "I think too when a youngster asks a philosophical question do not try to answer it for them. Instead say 'well, that is interesting, what do you think?' We are all inquirers together on this."

Batting a question back may not be the approach that children find the easiest. Especially as they progress through the education system, they may insist that there are rational, tangible answers to everything, and press you hard for precise answers to questions of great mystery. As humans we have a keen desire to find order, pattern, and law in the world, and when this drive dominates it can reduce our experience of life in its fullness. And somewhere along the line as we grow up, we may stop asking those big important questions, and I don't think it's because we have already got the answers sussed. "I do think that this kind of questioning can be encouraged or discouraged. It seems to be that children are natural inquirers. Much of what happens in their interaction with adults takes this away," says Pat Hannam. Professor Fisher agrees: "My research shows that as children grow older they ask fewer questions in school. If it is not encouraged this natural curiosity dies and many children come to believe that in life it is others who ask the questions."

HOW TO KEEP YOUR CHILDREN THINKING THOSE BIG THOUGHTS

- *Affirm your children's questions.* Says Professor Fisher, "Adults can encourage questioning by actively welcoming questions, through saying, for example, 'That's an interesting question,' and by taking time to listen and respond to their children's questions."
- *Invite thoughtful questions about the day.* Ask your children whether they have had any interesting thoughts during their day or asked any interesting questions at school.

- *Use books and television as a springboard for thinking.* "You encourage an inquiring mind by asking children interesting questions about characters in books or on TV, such as 'I wonder why he/she did/thought that?'" says Professor Fisher.
- *Don't be judgmental about your children's questions.* If you tell a child that his question is silly, then he may lose his confidence to ask more.
- *Offer questions back to your children.* Resist the temptation to answer your children immediately, and instead encourage them to explore their own question further. "Try not to tell children what to think but ask them what they think, then share with them what you think," advises Professor Fisher.
- *Don't be critical about your children's answers.* If you think your child's answer to a question is misguided, avoid being judgmental and instead encourage her to reflect further. "A good follow-up is to ask 'Why do you think that?'" says Professor Fisher.
- *Allow room for different views.* When it comes to matters of belief, frame your answer subjectively with "No one knows for sure, but I believe . . ." Says Professor Fisher, "Try to ensure a balance of views between you and your child."
- *Don't be afraid to say "I don't know."* You don't have to have all the answers!

MAKE A CONVERSATION JAR OR BASKET[1]

This lovely, simple idea came to me in a newsletter from Meg Cox, a writer who is interested in family ritual. She and her family have come up with a novel way to encourage thoughtful conversation at mealtimes. "We have a conversation basket. There are three strings of beads hanging down from the top handle with the words 'Talk, Talk, Talk' on them, and inside the basket are colored slips of paper with questions. Every night at dinner, we each pick one piece of paper and answer that question. Then the others get a crack at it. The most popular questions so far include: 'If you could change places with one other person alive today, who would it be?' and 'Who makes you laugh?' To keep from running out of questions, there are blank papers in the basket and anyone can add a question whenever it occurs to him or her. This simple addition to dinner has made a positive difference, leading to all sorts of fun digressions."

Teach Children about
Life and Death

When we shy away from death, the ever-changing nature of things, we inevitably shy away from life.

M. SCOTT PECK, *The Road Less Traveled*

THE OTHER DAY, on the way home from school, my children and I found a dead fox on the side of the road. We gathered around the motionless creature for at least ten minutes, seizing the opportunity to have a long look at a beautiful fox close up. We marveled at its bushy tail, its vibrant chestnut color, its tongue lolling out of its mouth and, finally, its eyes, slightly open, dull and empty. We speculated about how it had died, and then I said a brief prayer of thanks for the animal's life. None of us could quite believe that the fox would not suddenly jump up and run for cover, or even bite our noses. Perhaps all it takes is a sudden "Boo!" suggested my youngest. It is hard for all of us to understand how life can disappear; as Shakespeare's Othello said when comparing the murder of his wife to the extinguishing of a flame, "I know not where is that Promethean heat / That can thy light relume." Death is an especially difficult concept for children, who, psychologists believe, do not have the cognitive ability to understand its finality until at least the age of six. Karen, the mother to three sons, noticed that it was at this age that all her children suddenly went through a phase when they were curious about death. "They all became obsessed with it," she remembers. "They would ask difficult questions, like 'when will I die?' or ask me when I will die. I have tried to be as honest as I can without frightening them. I tell them that no one knows when we will die, but we hope that we will live for a very long time, and most of us do."

Many parents, understandably, want to protect their children from knowledge about death. We all want our little loved ones to inhabit a happy, positive world, but it seems to me that to deny them the reality of death also denies them something of the reality of life. If we do not allow the concept of death to gently permeate their lives, they will be ill prepared if sudden tragedy were to strike. As the opening quotation to this chapter suggests, death also offers us the best opportunity we have to consider the value and meaning of our lives. As a spiritual parent we will be eager to make sure that our children's education about death is imparted with sensitivity and wisdom.

The modern child's relationship to death is likely to be a puerile one. Many children are exposed to high levels of glorified violence and death through television, movies, and video games. At Halloween they play ghoulish games to confront fears about what lies beyond the grave. However, most children are unlikely to have ever seen a real dead body, or possibly even to have had a meaningful conversation with an adult about our final destiny. Sex education is given a high profile on the school curriculum, but education about death is minimal, as it is in our wider society, where it is only whispered about. Such is the taboo that surrounds death. Who has heard of thanatology? This almost unrecognized term means the study of death, something that we all eventually experience, but few deem worthy of inquiry.

It is important that we share with our children the deeper meanings of death, not in a morbid, fearful way, but as a natural process and great mystery. For the spiritual parent this will mean talking about the cycles of life and the possibility of an afterlife.

EXPLAINING DEATH TO CHILDREN

Opportunities to discuss death with your child will spontaneously occur in your lives together. On the simplest level you can point out to your children the cycles of birth and death that exist in nature. Notice together how flowers first bloom and then die, how leaves bud into fullness and then drop, how autumn and winter follow spring and summer. Discuss the aging process by observing the changes in physiology between old and young; and, like the fox we found on the roadside, there are likely be animal corpses to contemplate. The death of a pet often provides children with their first experience of personal grief, and for this reason is a positive learning opportunity. If the child was very involved in the pet's life, the experience may be particularly sad. Karen says that the death of short-lived pets like hamsters and goldfish have been very useful opportunities to help her explain death to her three sons, age seven, ten, and twelve. But the death of these little creatures has also brought up profound and perplexing questions. "My son asked where his hamster had gone, and I had to say that I honestly didn't know. I think it's better to be honest with them." Although, like Karen, you may be stumped for answers, it's essential to create a culture in the home where death can be talked about. If you can pass on the message that death is a natural process, this is good preparation for losses more painful than fish and hamsters that are bound to come. The death of grandparents or other elderly relatives may also be a normal part of a child's growing up, striking a sad blow, especially if they had enjoyed a close and loving relationship.

Personal beliefs vary, but you may want to share with your children an assurance that death is not only an ending, but also a metamorphosis. All spiritual traditions teach that there is a part of the deceased that lives on in some way: this may be in our hearts and our memories or in some other heavenly realm; as a flux of consciousness and energy in nature; or as a new, reborn life. The challenge is to find ways to share this understanding with children that are in tune with their developmental level. Here are some phrases that may be helpful:

"Granddad has gone to heaven to be with God."

"We can't see granddad anymore, but he lives on inside us, in our hearts."

"Part of granddad lives on in all life around us: in the trees, birdsong, grass, wind, and stars."

Simple metaphors may help you explain death to older children. You could talk about how leaves fall off the tree to return to their roots; or how a ship sails out of our sight when it goes beyond the horizon (see also box on page 200).

There are many children's books now on the market about death and bereavement, and reading a well-chosen one together is likely to be very helpful and healing.

I think it's important to set our life-after-death beliefs within the context of unknowing. Parents do not have absolute answers: it is a mystery that we do our best to understand. We need to let our children know that people have different ideas about what happens to us after we die, and that what we are offering them is our own personal understanding on the matter.

These two simple activities may help children understand the concept of death and possible afterlife.

THE ICE CUBE LESSON

Take a bowl of water with ice cubes in it. Explain that each ice cube represents a living person or animal. The surrounding water is God or Spirit. The ice cubes are made up of the surrounding water, only in solid physical form. When we die we give up our physical body, like the melting ice cubes, and return to the source from which we came.

THE HAND IN GLOVE LESSON

Hold out your hand and wriggle it, explaining that this is our spirit, the bit of us that is with God before we are born. When we arrive on Earth we take on a physical body—put on a glove and wriggle your hand. When we die our spirit leaves our body—take off the glove and lay it down. The spirit goes back to God, our source—wriggle your hand.

CHILDREN AND BEREAVEMENT

Children experience bereavement as intensely as adults, but may express it in different ways. A policy statement issued by The American Academy of Pediatrics lists thirty-six possible manifestations of grief: crying, clinging behavior, regression, disobedience, physical illness, sleep problems, or apparently seeming unmoved are just some of those listed. A child's grief evolves over time, and varies enormously. Children under six can convince themselves that the death was punishment vented on them, or that they are in some way responsible for it. Children need to be reassured that it's not their fault. Whether it's a pet that has died or a close relative, counselors agree that children need to be given plenty of opportunity to talk about their loss, and be able to share memories of their loved one. Pictures can be drawn, poems written, photos assembled into montages to help children express their feelings. They often also need to be reassured that they themselves are not at risk of suddenly dying, nor are other people who are close to them.

On funerals, the general consensus is that it is beneficial for children to attend them, or, if this might prove to be too traumatic, at least given the opportunity to engage in some ritual of good-bye. When the father of one of my friends' children died, I was much moved at the way she got her two boys, then aged five and seven, to decorate their dad's coffin with photos, pictures, and mementos. Helen Fitzgerald, a pioneering death educator in the United States, advocates a short memorial service for children conducted prior to the funeral, in which age-appropriate readings, prayers, songs, and activities can be used. I especially like her idea of getting children to launch biodegradable helium balloons on which are written good-bye messages.

Spiritual parents may be reassured to hear about a piece of research published in the *British Medical Journal*. The study found that adults who have strong spiritual beliefs resolve their grief more quickly and more completely than those who don't. The spiritual adults took up to fourteen months to reach a resolution, while those without a faith took longer. Let's hope the same may also be true for children raised in a spiritual home.

Remember that Childhood Doesn't Last Forever

In my beginning is my end.

T.S. ELIOT, *Four Quartets*

PARENTS WITH OLDER children often tell me how quickly their children grew up. Looking back, they never know where all the time went. This may be a hard perspective to identify with when we are shivering on the sidelines of our son's football training, or trying to scrape off the dried food embedded in the highchair. Time can move at snail speed when we are engaged in some of the humdrum aspects of parenting, but it is enriching to hold in mind the transitory nature of it all.

There comes a time when our baby doesn't want the breast anymore; when our preschooler no longer has chubby legs; when our seven-year-old doesn't giggle at our silly faces; when our ten-year-old doesn't want to hold our hand; when our thirteen-year-old no longer has a child's body.

The notion of impermanence is core to Buddhist thinking. According to Buddhists nothing is permanent or stable; it is in fact always dying. This is good news because with death comes change and without that life would not be possible. Our children could not grow up into fine adults if there weren't impermanence. We are on loan to each other only for a short while. We can never bathe twice in the same river, said the Greek philosopher Heraclitus, nor can we dip into this moment of our parenthood twice, no matter how beautiful the experience. Look at those old baby photographs and video recordings: are they not already tinged with the sepia of nostalgia? Have we not captured so many images of our children precisely because we know that time does move on and our children change and grow at a rapid speed.

During an Ash Wednesday service, Christians mark their foreheads with a sign of the cross in ash to remind themselves that from dust we come and to dust we shall return. Parents may benefit from imagining that we are wearing our own ash mark on our foreheads, not to be morbid but to remind ourselves that this time we have with our children will have an end. If we look deeply into the fleeting nature of our journey together as parent and child we will do our best to be joyful, right now. That school summer vacation may not seem so long and troubling when we realize that each sunny or wet day counts away a precious, and very short, childhood.

INDEPENDENCE

Our children are continually making steps toward independence. It is something they both welcome and fear. They are excited about starting school, but then when it comes time to say goodbye, they are stuck to our legs like limpets. As parents we have a responsibility to encourage children to make steps toward independence—from learning to walk and brush their teeth, to being responsible for their schoolwork, friends, and money. Sometimes they will take a step forward, and sometimes we may need to take a step quietly back. I can remember that as a child I was terrified of swimming. After a school crash course I was the only child who still would not take her feet off the bottom. Eventually my dad took me swimming on Saturday mornings. He would float me in the water, and I would let myself swim only with the reassurance that his hand was under my tummy. "Your hand's still there, isn't it, Dad?" I'd ask, doing my best at the crawl. Then one day he broke the wonderful news to me: he had stopped putting his hand under my stomach and I had been swimming solo.

TRUST

When is the time right to pull away our supporting hand? We scrutinize our child's capabilities and then, finally, we take a deep intake of breath and trust. The water in the pool will hold up our beloved, that's the way life is.

We do our best as parents to give our children all that they need to blossom into fullness. It's a daunting task and one that we won't get perfectly right but, thankfully, we do not do the job alone, and nor are our children alone when they launch out from us. There is, and always will be, grace, the spirit of life, inviting us to be filled with love and hope and joy. It calls our children into life, just as the sun beckons a seedling growing on the windowsill to turn its leaves toward the sky. And if ever we doubt this age-old wisdom, we may unexpectedly get the shot of proof that we need. On a sunny day last weekend, my husband was driving our children to grandma's house. My eldest, age seven, was gazing out of the window when he suddenly announced. "I'm so happy, Daddy. Everything is so beautiful and I am so happy."

SPIRITUAL PRACTICE FOR PARENTS

Imagine that your child has grown up and is about to leave home. Write a good-bye letter to her to wish her well. Let her know what you feel about her. Let her know what you hope you have given her in life to equip her for her journey. Let her know what you want for her in the world. What does this letter tell you about how you want to be parenting your child now, today?

LETTING GO

Each new step our children take toward independence is a birth, to be marked by smiles, hand-clapping, and photographs. It is also a little death, as we secretly grieve the loss of their need for us. There is an old saying that the first and last steps are the hardest.

The new schoolchildren may be crying in the classroom, but look too at how many parents have tears in their eyes as they walk alone out of the playground. As parents, we continually need to be letting go. This can be agonizing, especially when we are terrified that our children will make serious mistakes or be harmed by others. I know of a father who shadowed his daughter's first lone journey home from school in his car with binoculars. My mother swears she "never slept a wink" the whole time that I went traveling solo around India when in my twenties. Learning to let go is a process, as we transfer responsibility for children's lives from us to them. We have to make careful judgments about the inherent risks in a situation, and the capabilities of our children to deal with them. We need to set guidelines, establish limits, negotiate, be willing to let them get it wrong, and eventually we have to do our best to release them. This doesn't mean that we stop loving them. Our love for them is a flame inside that it is impossible to blow out; it is what will illuminate the journey we are required to make to that place where we can stand and wave and send our blessings in the wind. In the words of the poet Kahlil Gibran, "they are the sons and daughters of Life's longing for itself"; they belong not to us, but to the world.

Notes

INTRODUCTION
1. Aldous Huxley, *The Perennial Philosophy* (Perennial 1990).
2. Ken Wilber, *Grace and Grit* (Gill & Macmillan 1991).

1. MAKE THE DECISION TO PARENT WITH SPIRIT
1. Kahlil Gibran, *The Prophet* (Pan 1991).
2. C. J. Jung, *The Development of the Personality*, The Collected Works of C. G. Jung, Vol. 17 (Princeton University Press 1981).

2. RECOGNIZE YOUR CHILD'S NATURAL SPIRITUALITY
1. David Hay and Rebecca Nye, *The Spirit of the Child* (Zondervan 2002).
2. Ken Wilber, *Integral Psychology: Consciousness, Spirit, Psychology, Therapy* (Shambala Publications 2000).
3. Deepak Chopra, *The Seven Spiritual Laws of Success for Parents* (Rider 1997).

3. DISCOVER SACRED TIME IN A BUSY LIFE
1. Thich Nhat Hanh, *The Miracle of Mindfulness* (Rider 1991).
2. David Spangler, *Parent as Mystic, Mystic as Parent* (Putnam Publishing Group 1998).

4. CREATE A FAMILY CREED
1. Stephen R. Covey, *The 7 Habits of Highly Effective Families* (Simon & Schuster 1998).

5. PRAY WITH YOUR CHILDREN
1. If you want to explore further prayer with your children, see *Circle of Grace: Learning to Pray with and for Your Children* (Ballantine Books 2000).
2. From *My Very First Prayers* (Lion Publishing 2003).

3. From Starhawk, Diane Baker, Anne Hill, *Circle Round: Raising Children in Goddess Traditions* (Bantam Books 2000).
4. From Judith Merrell, *New Ideas for Creative Prayer* (Scripture Union).

6. PRACTICE PARENTS' PRAYER
1. Deepak Chopra, *How to Know God: The Soul's Journey into the Mystery of Mysteries* (Rider 2001).

7. MEDITATE WITH YOUR CHILDREN
1. Caroline Mann, "Meditation in Education: Are children in the optimum state for effective learning?" (Graduate School of Education, Bristol University 2000).
2. David Fontana and Ingrid Slack, *Teaching Meditation to Children* (Thorsons 2002).

8. CREATE HOME RITUALS
1. Joseph Campbell, *Myths to Live By: How We Re-create Ancient Legends in Our Daily Lives to Release Human Potential* (Compass Books 1993).

9. REDISCOVER TRADITIONAL RITUALS
1. Advent ritual published with the permission of Betsy Williams. It first appeared in Connections, a publication of the Church of the Larger Fellowship, Unitarian Universalist, Boston, MA.

10. CREATE RITUALS FOR THE SEASONS
1. Starhawk, Diane Baker, Anne Hill, *Circle Round: Raising Children in Goddess Traditions* (Bantam Books 2000).

12. SAY GRACE AT MEALTIMES
1. From Mary Oliver, *New   Selected Poems* (Beacon Press 1992).
2. Sabrina Dearborn, *A Child's Book of Blessings* (A Barefoot Poetry Collection 1999).
3. Lois Rock, *My Very First Prayers* (Lion Publishing 2003).

13. HOLD FAMILY MEETINGS
1. David Robinson, *The Family Cloister: Benedictine Wisdom for the Home* (Crossroad Publishing Company 2000).

14. MAKE STORY TIME MAGIC
1. C. S. Lewis, *The Chronicles of Narnia* (Collins 2002); Frances Hodgson Burnett, *The Secret Garden* (Puffin Classics 1994); Phillipa Pearce, *Tom's Midnight Garden* (Puffin Books 1976); Eleanor H. Porter, *Pollyana* (Puffin Classics 1994); L. Frank Baum, *The Wizard of Oz* (Penguin Popular Classics 1995).

NOTES

2. David Almond, *Skellig* (Hodder Children's Books 1999); Sue Welford, *Waiting for Mermaids* (Oxford University Press 2002).
3. Martin Waddell, *The Big Big Sea* (Walker Books 1996); Sam McBratney, *Guess How Much I Love You* (Walker Books 2001); Marcus Pfister, *The Rainbow Fish* (North-South Books 2001); Margery Williams, *The Velveteen Rabbit* (Methuen Young Books 1995); Oscar Wilde, *The Selfish Giant* (Puffin Books 1982).
4. Words of Discovery, Unit 33, Vulcan House, Vulcan Road, Leicester LE5 3EF (tel: 01162 622244; Web site: www.wordsofdiscovery.com).
5. For collections of spiritual stories from around the world see: Hugh Lupton, *Tales of Wisdom and Wonder* (Barefoot Books 1998) and Margaret Silf, *100 Wisdom Stories From Around the World* (Lion Publishing 2003).
6. On the North American Web site Beliefnet many teaching tales from around the world are freely available. Go to www.beliefnet.com and visit the family and parenting archive.
7. Marcus Borg, *The God We Never Knew* (HarperSanFrancisco 1998).
8. Nancy Mellon, *Storytelling With Children* (Hawthorn Press 2000).

15. USE VISUALIZATION WITH YOUR CHILDREN
1. For further reading about visualization see Dina Glouberman, Life Choices and Life Changes Through Imagework (Unwin Hyman 1989).
2. In Maureen Garth, *Earthlight: New Meditations for Children* (Newleaf 1997).

16. GET CREATIVE
1. Julia Cameron, *The Artist's Way* (Pan Paperback 1995).
2. Matthew Fox, *Creativity: Where the Divine and the Human Meet* (Jeremy P. Tarcher 2002).

17. BE BODY AWARE
1. If you are looking for a yoga video to use with your children, try Barbara Currie's *Fun Yoga for Kids* (Video Collection Int. Ltd).
2. For a tai'chi book to use with children, try Stuart Alve Olson, *Tai'chi for Kids* (Bear & Co. 2001).

18. ENJOY THE SPIRIT OF PLAY
1. David Spangler, *Parent as Mystic, Mystic as Parent* (Putnam Publishing Group 1998).
2. Marcus Borg, *The God We Never Knew* (HarperSanFrancisco 1998).
3. For a family holiday with a nondenominational spiritual dimension, check out the family experience weeks organized by:
a) The Findhorn Foundation, a major international center for spiritual

education in northeast Scotland (The Park, Findhorn, Forres, Moray IV36 3TZ, Scotland, tel: 01309 690311, Web site: www.findhorn.org); b) Monkton Wyld Court, a holistic education center (Charmouth, Bridport, Dorset DT6 6DQ, tel: 01297 560342, Web site: www.monktonwyldcourt.org).

19. PRACTICE LOVING FAMILY DISCIPLINE
1. M. Scott Peck, *The Road Less Traveled* (Rider 1985).
2. For more thoughts about the principles of Taoism and discipline see David Carroll, *Spiritual Parenting: A Loving Guide for New Age Parents* (Paragon House Publishers 1990).

20. MAKE A SACRED SPACE IN YOUR HOME
1. For further reading on home altars see Denise Linn, *Altars: Bringing Sacred Shrines into Your Everyday Life* (Rider 1999).

21. CHOOSE TOYS WITH CARE
1. From David Carroll, *Spiritual Parenting: A Loving Guide for New Age Parents* (Paragon House Publishers 1990).

22. CONSIDER YOUR FAMILY'S MEDIA HABITS
1. Martin Large, *Set Free Childhood: Parents' Survival Guide for Coping with Computers and TV* (Hawthorne Press 2003).

23. PRACTICE ANIMAL CARE
1. For more thoughts on the spiritual lessons to be found in animal care, see Susan Chernak McElroy, Animal Grace: Entering a spiritual relationship with our fellow creatures (New World Library 2000).

25. USE NATURE AS A SPIRITUAL TEACHER
1. For further information see Theodore Roszak (ed.), Ecopsychology (Sierra Club Books 1995).
2. Theodore Roszak, *The Voice of the Earth* (Phanes Press 2002).
3. For organized nature-based family activities try: a) The Sierra Club (tel: 415-977-5500, Web site: www.sierraclub.org). b) The National Wildlife Federation (tel: 800-822-9919, Web site: www.nwf.org).
4. Joseph Cornell, *Sharing Nature with Children* (Dawn Publications 1998). Visit Joseph Cornell's Sharing Nature Foundation Web site at www.sharingnature.com.
5. For resources on stargazing the BBC and Open University has a site called Final Frontier, with monthly star maps. Visit www.open2net/science/finalfrontier/stargazing_index.htm.
6. The Windows to the Universe Web site (www.windows.ucar.edu/) has an archive of mythological sky stories.

7. John R. Stowe, *The Findhorn Book of Connecting With Nature* (Findhorn Press 2003).

26. SEEK OUT KINDRED SPIRITS
1. Robert Putnam, *Bowling Alone* (Simon & Schuster 2001).
2. Margaret Wheatley, *Turning to One Another* (Berrett-Koehler 2002).
3. For information on wisdom circles see Christine Baldwin, *Calling the Circle: The First and Future Culture* (Bantam Books 1998) and Charles Garfield, Cindy Spring, Sedonia Cahill, *Wisdom Circles: A Guide to Self-discovery and Community Building in Small Groups* (Hyperion 1999).

28. ENCOURAGE CHILDREN'S BIG QUESTIONS
1. The conversation jar idea is used with the permission of Meg Cox and first appeared in Meg Cox, *The Book of New Family Traditions* (Running Press 2003).

Further Reading
and Resources

Books
Books that have helped me in my research, and for which I am grateful, include:

Mimi Doe with Marsha Walch, *10 Principles for Spiritual Parenting* (HarperCollins 1998).
Peggy J. Jenkins, *Nurturing Spirituality in Children* (Beyond Words Publishing 1995).
Linda Kavelin Popov, *The Family Virtues Guide* (Penguin Books USA 1997).
Steven M. Rosman, *Spiritual Parenting* (Quest Books 1994).

Useful Web sites
www.beliefnet.com
  North American articles and columns on spirituality and world religion.
www.childspirit.net
  A North American organization dedicated to understanding and nurturing the spirituality of children.
www.pcnbritain.org.uk
  A British ecumenical network promoting a progressive and open Christian understanding.

If you would like to contact Jane Bartlett or explore further the ideas shared in this book, visit: www.parentingwithspirit.co.uk.

Permissions

The author would like to thank the following for permission to quote copyright material: Beacon Press for lines from "Rice" by Mary Oliver, from *New and Selected Poems by Mary Oliver*, copyright 1992 by Mary Oliver, reprinted by permission of Beacon Press, Boston; EMI Longitude Music/EMI Music Publishing Ltd for lines from "Celebration," words and music by Robert Earl Bell, Ronald Nathan Bell, George Melvin Brown, Robert Mickens, James Taylor, Dennis Ronald Thomas, Earl Eugene Toon, Jr., Eumir Deodeta, Claydes Eugene Smith, copyright 1980 EMI Longitude Music/EMI Music Publishing Ltd, London WC2H 0QY; Prayer from *Circle Round* by Starhawk, Diane Baker, and Anne Hill, copyright 2000 by Miriam Simas, Anne Hill, and Diane Baker, reprinted by permission of Bantam Books, a division of Random House Inc.; Bob Dylan lyrics from "Blowin' in the Wind," words and music by Bob Dylan, copyright 1962 by Special Rider Music, Sony/ATV Music Publishing Ltd.

Every effort has been made to contact all copyright owners but if any have been inadvertently overlooked the author and publishers will be pleased to make the necessary arrangement at the first opportunity.

Index

A
Aboriginal tradition, 95, 124
Acibar, Pip, 118
"active imagination," 103
adolescence, 15
Advent, celebrating, 63–4
advertising, 153
age and stages
    meditation, 52
    musical training, 111
    prayers, 34, 120–1
aggression. *see also* violence
    channeling, 119
aggressive toys, 147–8
Agombar, Marian, 29
Alexander, C. F., 159
All Saints Day, 75
All Souls' Day, 75
altars. *see* home altars
American Heart association, 116
American Heart Journal, 44
ancestors, 76
Anglicans, xii, 182
animal care, 159–63
animal cruelty, 161
anthology of prayers, 39–40
anxiety, visualization and, 105–6
arts
    cartoons violence, 152
    encouraging creativity in, 110
    marital, 118–19
Ashtanga, 118
Ash Wednesday, 203
Assagioli, Roberto, 103
"attachment parenting," 13

"attunement," 17, 21
authoritarian parents, 132
autumn altars, 72
autumn equinox, 72
awareness
    achieving, 18
    body, 10, 115–21
    children and, 9–10
    of movement, 120

B
babies, 12–13, 115, 172
Baker, Diane, 72
baptism, 171
bat hunt, 76
Baum, L. Frank, 93
"beauty walks," 178
bedtime
    guided visualization for, 104–5
    prayers, 34, 37
    quiet time, 165–6
    stories, 92
behavior (positive), prayer and, 33
Benedict, St., 165
Benedictines, 89, 165
bereavement, children and, 200–1
Bible
    on body awareness, 116
    seeking reconciliation and, 133
    stories, 95
    visualization and, 106
biogenetics, 56
"biophilia," 172
birthday candle ritual, 77
birthdays, 76